# AIR
# WARFARE

## Air Force Doctrine Document 3-1
## 22 January 2000

Incorporating Change 1, 28 July 2011

This document complements related discussion found in Joint Publication 3-0, *Doctrine for Joint Operations*

BY ORDER OF THE
SECRETARY OF THE AIR FORCE

AIR FORCE DOCTRINE DOCUMENT 3-1
22 JANUARY 2000
INCORPORATING CHANGE 1, 28 JULY 2011 |

## SUMMARY OF CHANGES

This Interim change to Air Force Doctrine Document (AFDD) 2-1, changes the cover to AFDD 3-1, *Air Warfare* to reflect revised AFI 10-1301, Air Force Doctrine (9 August 2010). AFDD numbering has changed to correspond with the joint doctrine publication numbering architecture. AFDD titles and content remain unchanged until updated in the next full revision. A margin bar indicates newly revised material.

OPR: LeMay Center/DD
Certified by: LeMay Center/DD (Col Todd C. Westhauser)
Pages: 116
Accessibility: Available on the e-publishing website at www e-publishing.af mil for
            downloading
Releasability: There are no releasability restrictions on this publication
Approved by: LeMay Center/CC, Maj Gen Thomas K. Andersen, USAF
            Commander, LeMay Center for Doctrine Development and Education

# FOREWORD

Since the Wright Brothers first flew at Kitty Hawk, the airplane has continually evolved as an instrument of military and national power. *Today, the proper employment of aerospace power is essential for success on and over the modern battlefield.* In many instances it will be the military power of choice. Future advances in stealth, precision, and lethality will make aerospace power increasingly more effective at all levels of warfare across the range of military operations. Airmen must not only understand the employment of aerospace power, but be able to articulate the principles of air warfare.

Operation DESERT STORM (1991) validated the concept of a campaign in which aerospace power, applied simultaneously against strategic and operational centers of gravity (COGs), rendered opposing military forces virtually ineffective. Aerospace power emerged as a dominant form of military might. It was decisive primarily because it achieved paralysis of the enemy at all levels of war with minimal casualties to friendly forces. Recent events in Bosnia (1995) and Kosovo (1999) continue to re-validate that air warfare, using aerospace power and a joint air operations plan (JAOP), will continue to be an essential and sometimes decisive tool in future military operations. Air Force Doctrine Document 2-1, *Air Warfare*, provides a basis for understanding, planning, and executing air warfare.

The US Air Force has adopted the term *"aerospace"* to describe the medium within which its forces operate and has applied the term to those broad and enduring concepts that apply across the entire medium. The separate terms *"air"* and *"space"* continue to be used when describing those specific tasks, missions, or platforms that apply strictly to the air or space environment.

**MICHAEL E. RYAN**
**General, USAF**
**Chief of Staff**

**22 January 2000**

i

# TABLE OF CONTENTS

# INTRODUCTION

*Air power has become predominant, both as a deterrent to war, and—in the eventuality of war—as the devastating force to destroy an enemy's potential and totally undermine his will to wage war.*

**General Omar Bradley**

## PURPOSE

This Air Force Doctrine Document (AFDD) implements Air Force Policy Directive (AFPD) 10-13, *Air and Space Doctrine*. AFDD 2-1 *Air Warfare* establishes operational doctrine for air warfare. It provides initial guidance for conducting air operations as part of aerospace warfare. Specifically, this document contains beliefs and principles that guide the organization, command and control, employment, and support of air forces conducting wartime operations. It examines relationships among objectives, forces, environments, and actions that enhance the ability of air operations to contribute to achieving assigned objectives. It focuses on the sequencing of events and the application of forces and resources to ensure aerospace power makes useful contributions to military and national objectives. It examines the importance of command relationships, intelligence, space, logistics, and other factors to the planning and conduct of air warfare.

## APPLICATION

This AFDD applies to all Air Force military and civilian personnel (includes Air Force Reserve Command [AFRC] and Air National Guard [ANG] units and members). The doctrine in this document is authoritative but not directive. Therefore, commanders need to consider not only the contents of this AFDD, but also the particular situation when accomplishing the mission.

This document supports the fundamental concept of a single commander who is responsible for the planning and conduct of aerospace warfare in a theater of operations. This single commander is codified in joint doctrine as the joint force air component commander (JFACC).

## SCOPE

**This document focuses on the operational and strategic maneuver aspects of air warfare in theater and global operations.** This document does not specifically address military operations other than war (MOOTW), but the doctrinal guidance in this document can be applied to MOOTW where appropriate. Furthermore, this document also does not specifically address airlift, but many portions apply to airlift as part of an overall air operation. Other doctrine documents provide specific guidance on MOOTW and airlift operations. Additional information on Air Warfare may be found in subordinate operational- and tactical-level doctrine.

# CHAPTER ONE

# AIR WARFARE FUNDAMENTALS

*To conquer the command of the air means victory; to be beaten in the air means defeat and acceptance of whatever terms the enemy may be pleased to impose.*

**Giulio Douhet**

## STRATEGY

**Strategy is a means to accomplish an end.** Since overall theater strategy for employment of US forces is normally developed jointly, it is imperative that aerospace power be properly represented at the highest levels of strategy development. It is not prudent to wait for a theater strategy, emphasizing surface maneuver to be developed, and then create a supporting air strategy. There are opportunities for a balanced, integrated strategy to be developed, and in some cases, an effective air-centric approach at the theater level would be an optimum use of available forces. But without adequate air and space expertise at that level, planning has historically devolved to an emphasis on surface warfare operations and objectives and how they can be supported by aerospace power. *This does not imply that aerospace power is the answer in every case, but it does mandate that theater-level planning include examining aerospace power options from the beginning.*

*Strategy is the employment of battle to gain the end in war; it must therefore give an aim to the whole military action, which must be in accordance with the object of the war; in other words, strategy forms the plan of the war.*

**Carl von Clausewitz**

## THE JOINT FORCE COMMANDER'S (JFC) CAMPAIGN

**The JFC's campaign is a series of major operations that arrange tactical, operational, and strategic actions to accomplish strategic and operational objectives.** Wartime campaigns integrate air, land, sea, space and special operations, interagency and multinational operations in harmony with diplomatic, economic, and informational efforts to attain national and multinational objectives.

1

Air operations involve the employment of air assets by themselves or in concert with other assets or forces and are part of the overall joint campaign. They can be used as the primary focus of the JFC's theater campaign plan, as in Operation ALLIED FORCE, or they can complement and reinforce the employment of other forces. No matter what type of air operation is used in the joint strategy, a joint air operations plan (JAOP) is the essential aerospace ingredient in the JFC's overall campaign plan. The JAOP links specific air and space objectives and tasks with overall military and political strategy. It also describes centers of gravity, phasing of operations, and resources required. It describes how aerospace power is used to achieve the overall theater and strategic objectives. It explains how other forces will support air and space operations, taking advantage of the synergism between aerospace and other forces. It also shows how air forces will complement and support other forces to achieve joint objectives. Like the overall theater plan, the JAOP carries through to the conclusion of the joint campaign and describes the desired end state.

## AIR OPERATIONS AND AEROSPACE STRATEGY

**Every JAOP should include a desired outcome, target set, and a mechanism for achieving the desired outcome.** The task of the air strategist is to translate a number of conflicting and competing targeting requirements into a workable JFC air operations plan that supports the overall joint campaign. This is done by first asking three fundamental questions: What is the goal? How much is it worth to achieve that goal? and What is it worth to the enemy to prevent friendly forces from achieving it? These are vital questions, and Bismarck's famous dictum, "Woe to the statesman whose reasons for entering a war are not as clear at the end as at the beginning," is absolutely correct. Once these basic

Weapons are the instruments of war: soldiers have rifles, seamen have ships, and airmen have aircraft. The AOC is the weapon of the JFACC through which he commands the joint aerospace forces.

questions are addressed, the strategist devises a joint campaign plan to answer them, with a joint force air operation as part of it. This involves transforming broad goals into specific military objectives, identifying the target sets that need to be affected (not necessarily destroyed) to attain those objectives, and then converting the whole into a coordinated operations order (OPORD) that can be implemented by the military forces involved. *It cannot be overemphasized that there must be a clear linkage between the targets chosen and the objectives sought.* If the overall objective is to force the enemy to halt an invasion of a neighboring country, then how, exactly, will striking the power grid—or munitions factory, or armored divisions, or intelligence headquarters—contribute towards achieving that objective? In other words, just because a target is destroyed or neutralized does not mean objectives were achieved. The process of linking ends and means is a critical requirement for the air strategist. The ultimate results are often psychological in nature; war is after all a human endeavor, and attempting to predict human reaction too precisely can be difficult. Nevertheless, understanding the links between cause and either physical or psychological effect is a key part of air warfare planning. *Failure to properly analyze the mechanism that ties tactical results to strategic effects has historically been the shortcoming of both airpower theorists and strategists.*

**Asymmetric Force Strategy**

**A number of developments in recent years have contributed to the emergence of a "new American way of war."** US military forces now employ sophisticated military capabilities to achieve national objectives and avoid costly force-on-force engagements that characterized the traditional strategies of attrition and annihilation that evolved from nineteenth century warfare. Airpower is particularly relevant to this new way of war or, as it is commonly referred to, "asymmetric force strategy." Asymmetric force strategy dictates applying US strengths against adversary vulnerabilities and enabling the US to directly attack an enemy's centers of gravity (COGs) without placing Americans or allies at risk unnecessarily. Five key components of asymmetric force strategy are:

✪ **The commander's conceptualization of the battlespace** uses information to conceive a strategy for employment. It includes collecting and exploiting the information necessary to identify threats and opportunities regarding national interests and preparing the area of concern to initiate and conduct operations. This is a key step to perform before committing resources to an operation. A key part of maintaining consistency in this effort is intelligence preparation of the battlespace (IPB).

○ **Controlling the battlespace** means exercising the degree of control necessary in all media (land, sea, and aerospace, in both their physical and information domains) to employ, maneuver, and engage forces while denying the same capability to the adversary. To position forces and maximize the effectiveness of maneuver for decisive effect, commanders should have freedom of operation. Forces and lines of communication should be protected from a diverse set of threats to obtain that freedom of action and to ensure the ability of friendly forces to deploy, maneuver, and engage an opponent. Battlespace control includes a number of active measures such as ensuring aerospace and maritime superiority. Furthermore, information superiority and control of the use of the electromagnetic spectrum also plays a critical role in battlespace control. *The form of battlespace control most often practiced by aerospace forces is air superiority, which enables friendly forces to use the air medium for military purposes while denying the enemy effective use of the same.*

○ **Decisive maneuver** is positioning forces to gain favorable advantages over an adversary or event in anticipation of engagement or strike. Maneuver is inherent in aerospace power. Decisive maneuver requires rapidly deployable, highly mobile joint forces that can outpace and outmaneuver opposing forces. These forces should be adept at sustained and integrated operations from dispersed postures. During operations, forces are positioned so they might rapidly transition to precision employment, applying appropriate combinations of lethal and nonlethal attacks against the enemy. The speed, range, and flexibility of air and space assets make them uniquely qualified to employ rapid maneuver against the enemy for maximum effect. *Aerospace power alone possesses the capability to bypass the bulk of enemy forces and maneuver directly to their vital targets, whether the targets be critical-fielded forces or key strategic centers.*

**Aerospace power's inherent ability to maneuver also lends itself to strategic mobility.** As the US Air Force adopts a more expeditionary posture, with air expeditionary forces (AEFs) on alert for contingency deployments, the ability to quickly deploy decisive combat power to trouble spots will become more important. Forward deployable aerospace combat power, along with continental US (CONUS)-based global power, is vital to the protection of US national interests.

4

✪ **Precision employment** is the direct application of force to degrade an adversary's capability or will, or the employment of forces to affect an event. Airpower assets can effectively engage the adversary on land, in the air, or at sea throughout the depth of the battlespace and can deny the enemy the use of space by attacking vital ground nodes such as launch and communications facilities. Precision employment includes the application of force and supplies to achieve the desired result, along with the required information to make that employment truly precise.

✪ **Integrated sustainment** is the ability to effectively deploy and maintain forces. Integrated sustainment includes logistics, readiness, facilities, and modernization.

A key part of asymmetric force strategy as employed by aerospace power is the concept of *parallel attack.* Parallel attack is defined as "simultaneous attack of varied target sets to shock, disrupt, or overwhelm an enemy, resulting in decisive effects. Parallel attack is possible at one or multiple levels of war and achieves rapid effects that leave the enemy little time to respond." Because of its speed, range, flexibility, and ability to maneuver as required to locate and precisely attack targets while neutralizing or avoiding threats, aerospace power is uniquely suited to conducting rapid, parallel attacks against the enemy. The three-dimensional maneuver capability of aerospace forces allows them to avoid noncritical enemy forces or defenses much more easily than surface forces. As figure 1.1 depicts, *air and space operations can support multiple simultaneous missions, and can easily flow from one phase, objective, or effect to the next as simply as changing targets for the next mission.*

## FUNCTIONS, EFFECTS, AND MISSIONS

Any discussion of the various aspects of air warfare requires a careful definition of the terms involved. In this regard, it is easy to become confused when comparing and contrasting the concepts of *function, effect, and mission.*

**AFDD 1 defines functions as the broad, fundamental, and continuing activities of aerospace power.** Examples include counterair, counterspace, countersea, counterland, strategic attack, counterinformation, etc. Functions are the means by which Services or components accomplish the tasks assigned by the JFC.

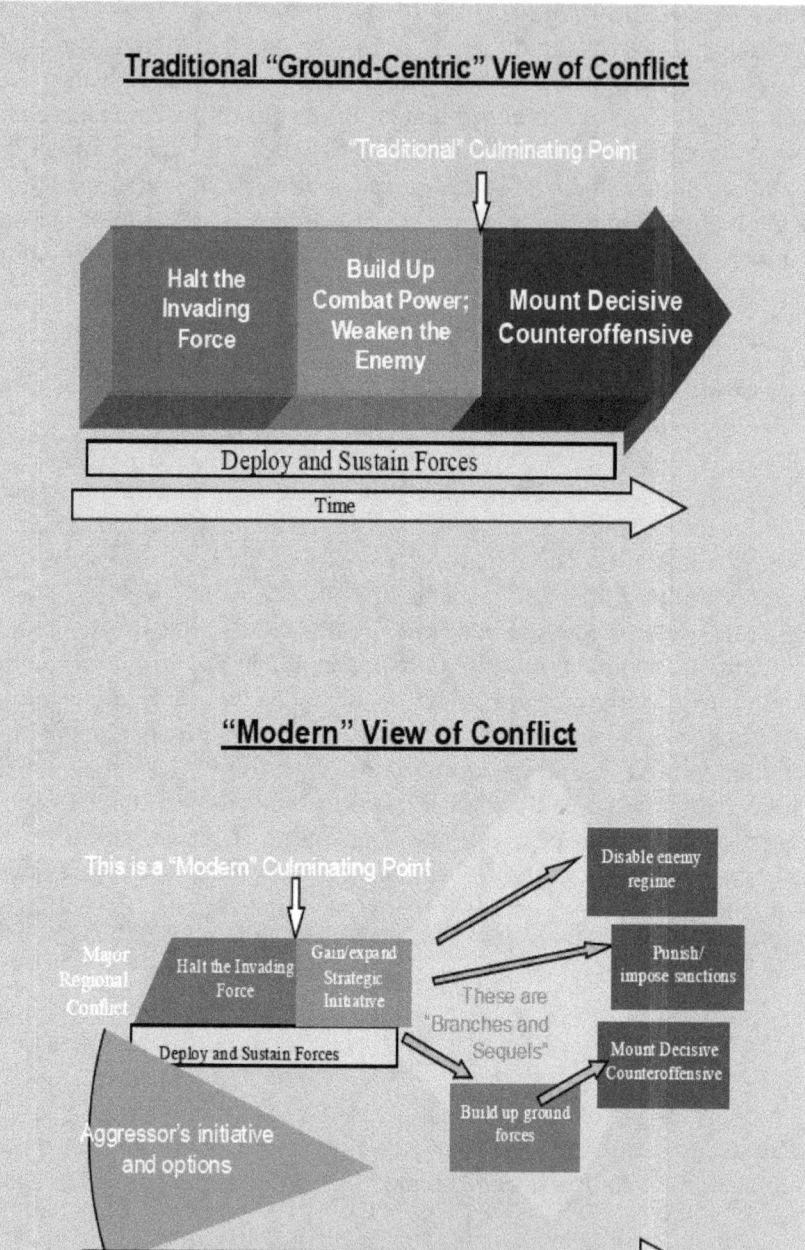

**Figure 1.1. Traditional Versus Modern Views of Conflict**

**Effects are the operational- or strategic-level outcomes that functions are intended to produce.** For example, a joint force air component commander (JFACC) employs the *function* of counterair to achieve the *effect* of aerospace superiority, or employs the counterland function to achieve the effect of battlefield isolation. The strategic attack function is often aimed directly at producing the strategic effect of enemy defeat, with no intermediate level effects on enemy forces involved.

Any discussion of effect must include the concepts of *direct* and *indirect* effects. Direct effects are those that result immediately from attacking the target set or sets involved. For example, bombing enemy surface-to-air missile (SAM) sites and the associated command and control (C2) facilities may directly result in SAM and radar sites destroyed, but the cumulative indirect effect may be to achieve aerospace superiority across the theater, which in turn allows other effects to be imposed on the enemy. Detailed analysis of interconnected indirect effects can easily become complex, and such effects are nearly impossible to predict exactly. General predictions, however, can be made that have successfully guided aerospace strategy in conflicts from World War II to Operation ALLIED FORCE (1999).

**Another point requiring clarification is the difference between strategic attack and strategic effect.** A strategic effect is the disruption of the enemy's strategy, ability, or will to wage war or carry out aggressive activity through destruction or disruption of their COGs or other vital target sets, including command elements, war production assets, fielded forces, and key supporting infrastructure. If an operation aims directly at those key targets whose destruction or disruption can cause strategic effects, it is a strategic attack. Strategic effects can also indirectly result from the actions of aerospace or surface forces at the lower levels of war. An example of the latter would be destruction of the enemy army on the battlefield, which in turn impairs the enemy strategy to the point where it is forced to cease fighting. In this latter case, the results from the tactical level of war are eventually felt at the strategic level. *A key difference between aerospace power and surface warfare is that aerospace forces can often strike directly at key target sets that have strategic results, without having to go through the process of drawn-out attrition at the tactical level of war. Analyzing the enemy for such critical targets is a fundamental part of aerospace warfare.*

The term *mission,* as applied to the tactical level of war, describes the task assigned to small units, flights or individual aircraft, missiles, or spacecraft (This is different than the *"mission"* of the Air Force.). Therefore, these missions describe the immediate, tactical results (e.g., an enemy aircraft shot down or a bridge destroyed) and focus at the level of the operator in the field and the specific tasks that must be performed. The emphasis is more on affecting the enemy than on the platforms or weapons employed for the task. For example, destroying an enemy munitions factory is a *strategic attack mission,* while employing the same asset to cut an enemy supply route is an *air interdiction mission.* Unless there is a thorough understanding of the aerospace functions, confusion can occur based on the names of these functions since some of them also apply to tactical missions, such as strategic attack and countersea. The following section briefly addresses US Air Force functions as listed in AFDD 1, and where applicable, further addresses the specific mission categories within each.

### Counterair

**Counterair consists of operations to attain and maintain a desired degree of air superiority by the destruction or neutralization of enemy forces.** Both offensive and defensive actions are involved. The former involves aggressively neutralizing enemy forces in-flight or the supporting infrastructure on the ground, while the latter describes reactively engaging enemy aerospace forces which have already launched on an offensive mission. *The speed, range, and three-dimensional vantage point of air and space platforms give them unique capabilities, as well as limitations, when compared to ground or naval forces.*

**Although often represented by the F-15 Eagle, counterair and air superiority involves many different aircraft from information and battle management to various strike aircraft. The effect of air superiority is often a systemic effort teaming technology, training, tactics, command and control, information, and people.**

- **Offensive counterair (OCA) missions use** offensive aerospace forces to destroy, disrupt, or limit enemy air and missile threats. OCA missions *proactively* target enemy airborne forces, or those forces and supporting infrastructure while on the ground. *Surface attack* missions represent the air-to-ground portion of OCA and disrupts or destroys selected targets including runways complexes; hardened aircraft shelters; petroleum, oils, and lubricants (POL) and munitions storage facilities, and C2 facilities used by the enemy air force. The air-to-air portion of OCA is further broken down into the missions of fighter sweep and escort. *Fighter sweep* employs air superiority fighters sweeping through a designated portion of enemy airspace to sanitize any enemy air-to-air threat, while *escort* puts the air superiority fighters in a direct support role protecting less air-to-air capable strike assets from enemy fighters. Modern multi-role fighters often practice *self-escort* through the mixed carriage of long-range air-to-air missiles along with their standard air-to-ground weapons loads. *Suppression of Enemy Air Defenses* (SEAD) is a primary OCA mission designed to neutralize, destroy, or temporarily degrade enemy surface based air defenses by destructive or disruptive means.

An EA–6B supporting the OCA function via the SEAD mission during Operation ALLIED FORCE.

- **Defensive counterair (DCA)** includes both active and passive measures to protect friendly forces and vital interests from enemy air and missile attacks. *Active* air defense missions use reactive air-to-air fighters or other assets placed on airborne or ground alert status to destroy attacking air and missile threats or to reduce their effectiveness against friendly forces and assets. *Passive* air defense includes all measures, other than active air defense, to minimize enemy effectiveness and includes dispersion, camouflage, concealment, and hardened shelters.

Although some DCA missions are normally scheduled when enemy air attack is expected, air-to-ground OCA is typically the best way to employ limited assets against an air threat because it employs concentration of effects. DCA tends to disperse the counterair effort and many missions do not actually engage the enemy since attacking aircraft have the initiative.

## Counterspace

**Counterspace is the function that attains and maintains space superiority.** The main objectives of counterspace operations are to allow friendly forces to exploit space capabilities, while negating the enemy's ability to do the same. Air, space, land, sea, or special operations forces can conduct them. Counterspace operations include both offensive and defensive components.

○ **Offensive counterspace (OCS)** missions destroy or neutralize an adversary's space capabilities through attacks on the various elements of an adversary's space systems. Specific effects of OCS include disruption, denial, degradation, deception, and destruction of enemy space systems. OCS missions may include surface-to-surface or air-to-surface attack on launch facilities or space C2 nodes, jamming satellite uplink and downlink frequencies, and could expand in the future to more active attacks on vehicles in space.

○ **Defensive counterspace (DCS)** missions protect US space-related systems and capabilities from enemy attack or interference. The objective of active DCS missions is to detect, track, identify, intercept, and neutralize or destroy enemy forces that threaten friendly space capability. Passive defenses protect and increase the survivability of friendly space forces and their products.

## Counterland

**Counterland involves those operations conducted to attain and maintain a desired degree of superiority over surface operations by the destruction or neutralization of enemy surface forces.** The main objectives of counterland are to dominate the surface environment and prevent the opponent from doing the same. Counterland can either be accomplished in direct or indirect support of large-scale ground operations, or can be carried out with minimal or no friendly ground forces in the area. When friendly ground forces are present, counterland tends to be more effective at greater distances from the ground battle where fratricide is not an issue and the enemy may be more vulnerable. In the latter case, counterland operations may represent the bulk of overall theater strategy. *The ultimate expression of this doctrine is the "decisive halt" in which the enemy is both stopped short of reaching their objective, which may be to* *engage friendly ground forces and/or take territory, and destroyed or disrupted to such a degree that continued fighting is no longer possible.* Missions that are used to perform counterland are air interdiction (AI) and close air support (CAS).

○ **Air interdiction** is a form of aerial maneuver that destroys, disrupts, diverts, or delays the enemy's surface military potential before it can be used effectively against friendly forces, or otherwise achieve its objectives. Typical targets for AI are lines of communication, supply centers, command and control nodes, or fielded forces. *Air interdiction planners typically look for targets that leverage the available air assets by creating significant disruptions of the enemy through attacks on relatively few targets.* Direct attack of fielded forces, one vehicle or artillery battery at a time, is possible but tends to be a less efficient use of aerospace power. Air interdiction is either performed as part of an overall theater-wide interdiction effort, which typically aims to isolate all or part of the battlefield from its source of support and reinforcement, or as a more local effort in response to the needs of ground combat. Whenever AI is flown in the vicinity of ground operations, the two achieve the greatest results when the efforts are integrated.

○ **Close air support** is the use of aerospace assets to directly support the ground force. CAS is flown against targets that are in close proximity to friendly forces; that proximity requires detailed integration between CAS missions and the fire and movement of surface forces. In this context, forces in "close proximity" are close enough to engage one another with organic weapons such as artillery. Enemy forces that are not within this range are more properly the targets of AI rather than CAS. *Long range weapons that do not bring a pre-*

**The A-10 Thunderbolt II, commonly known as the "Warthog." A-10 pilots earned a deadly reputation with Iraqi ground units during Operation DESERT STORM. Iraqi prisoner of war (POW) debriefs revealed that they feared only the B-52 strikes more than the ubiquitous A-10.**

*ponderance of fire to the battlefield, such as tactical ballistic missiles, are not used to set the maximum distance of "close proximity."* While CAS is not considered the most efficient mission for aerospace power, in critical ground combat situations it may be the most effective. Control of close air support is performed by Air Force personnel attached to the ground units being supported, working closely with their Army counterparts. *Tactical control of CAS always remains with the air component commander, not the ground commander.*

In general terms, CAS should only be used when the surface force cannot handle the enemy with organic firepower. This makes the requirement for CAS greater with light forces, such as airborne or amphibious units, and less for heavy units such as armored divisions.

---

**Synergies at the Battle of Khafji**

The Battle of Khafji was a critical event during the Gulf War and exemplified the potential advantages of teaming information systems with interdiction assets. On January 29, 1991, two Iraqi heavy divisions began moving towards allied forces near Al Khafji. Once detected by the joint surveillance, target attack radar system's (JSTARS) sensors and mission crew, coalition commanders quickly and decisively diverted airpower to counter the Iraqi offensive. In the three days and over 1,000 sorties that followed, the two Iraqi divisions were rendered ineffective. One Iraqi veteran described the coalition air attacks as causing more damage in 30 minutes than in eight years of the Iran-Iraq War.

Coupled with the capabilities of its mission crew, the technology on board JSTARS contributed in three critical ways. First, it located and tracked Iraqi armor columns, immediately passing this information to airborne strike aircraft. Second, it gave commanders at the tactical air control center (TACC) a significantly enhanced picture of the battlefield situation. Finally, it provided critical insights about the Iraqi's movements and intentions directly to coalition ground commanders throughout the Khafji operation.

Advanced information systems ensured that the coalition forces at the Battle of Khafji maintained a heightened sense of awareness throughout the operation. Information technologies identified the enemy's intent, combat units, and scheme of maneuver, thus enabling coalition commanders to divert assets and decisively employ their airpower.

*Airpower and the Iraqi Offensive at Kahfji*
**AFSAA CD-ROM**

## Countersea

Countersea is a collateral function that extends the application of Air Force power into the maritime environment. Specific countersea missions include surface warfare (antiship), undersea warfare (antisubmarine), sea surveillance, and aerial minelaying. Other aerospace power functions and missions, such as counterair and aerial refueling, can support maritime operations in the joint environment. *While these missions will typically operate in support of friendly naval forces, they may be employed independently when friendly naval forces are not in the area.*

One of the most successful sea-control strikes occurred off the east coast of New Guinea in March 1943. In that battle, known as the Battle of the Bismarck Sea, approximately one hundred Allied planes, including modified B-25s carrying five-hundred-pound bombs, attacked and successfully destroyed an entire Japanese convoy. Flying at one hundred feet above the ocean surface, American B-25s skipped their bombs across the water and into the hulls of these ships. At the battle's conclusion, 12 cargo ships and 4 Japanese destroyers were sunk or severely damaged.

**Dr. Donald D. Chipman**
*AIRPOWER: A New Way of Warfare (Sea Control)*
**Airpower Journal**
**Fall 1997**

## Counterinformation

Counterinformation is the function that seeks to establish information superiority through control of the information realm. Like counterair, counterinformation enables other functions and missions to occur and can be broken down into offensive and defensive actions. Many counterinformation actions directly achieve counterinformation objectives, while others are better seen as part of counterforce functions (as in the case of employing anti-radiation missiles to achieve SEAD effects on the enemy). Since the focus of air warfare planning is on achieving effects on the enemy, *the label placed on a given action is best determined by the combination of function performed and effect achieved, rather than by the type of weapon (information, electronic, or physical attack) used.* A good example of this is the broad area called electronic warfare, which performs actions in many categories including air warfare and information operations.

**A key part of counterinformation is "information attack."** *Information attack refers to those activities taken to manipulate or destroy an adversary's information or information system without necessarily changing visibly the physical entity within which it resides.* Although different from the conventional concepts of physical and electronic attack (EA), information attack can be an equally important part of air warfare.

In many cases, an attack on a specific target may have components of two or even all three forms of attack. Figure 1.2 illustrates this in more detail and shows the connection among physical, information, and electronic methods of attack and how they can interplay in the same action. Other cases may involve only one method at work.

### Strategic Attack

Strategic attack is defined as military action carried out against an enemy's COGs or other vital target sets, including command elements, war-production assets, and key supporting infrastructure. *It affects a level of destruction and disintegration of the enemy's military capacity to the point where the enemy no longer retains the ability or will to wage*

**First employed during Operation Allied Force, the B-2 Spirit Bomber combines stealth technology with precision munitions and provides the Joint Force an all-weather global attack capability.**

*war or carry out aggressive activity.* The term "strategic attack" also applies to the actual missions flown against strategic targets and is valid when the primary value of those targets to the enemy exists at the strategic level of war. *Whether a particular mission is labeled strategic should be based primarily on the expected effects on the enemy and not on the type of force used or the specific type of target attacked.*

### Command and Control

Command is the art of motivating and directing people and organizations into action to accomplish missions. Control is inherent in

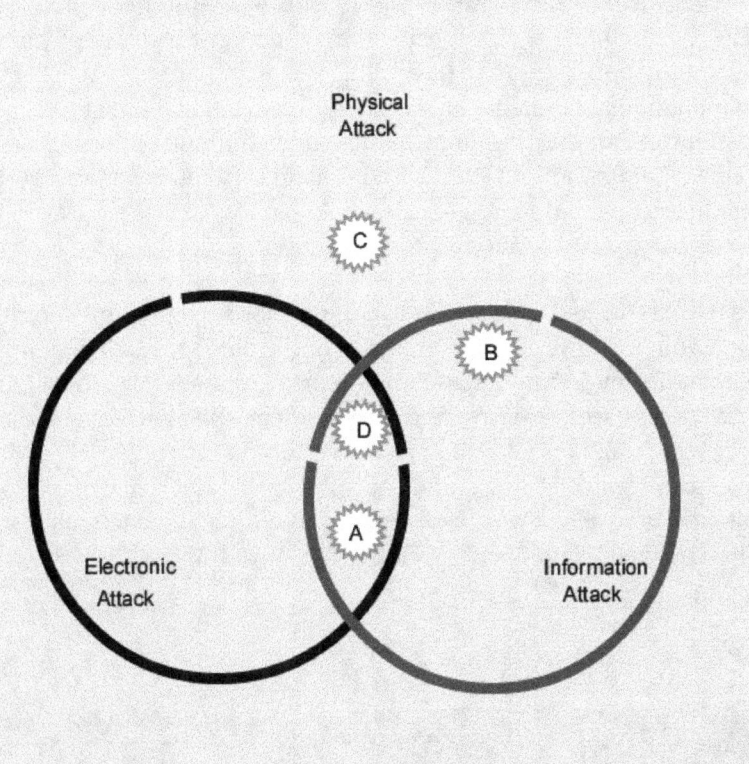

| | |
|---|---|
| A | Use of electromagnetic jamming to deny key information to the enemy. |
| B | Bombing an enemy C2 system represents both physical and information attack. |
| C | Perhaps the oldest use of airpower, physical attack of enemy forces or industrial production facilities represents pure physical attack. |
| D | An example of all three would be the use of a high-speed anti-radiation missile (HARM) to target the acquisition radar of an enemy surface-to-air missile (SAM) site for the purpose of obtaining local air superiority through SEAD. The HARM guides on the electronic emissions of the enemy radar, a form of electronic attack since it uses the electromagnetic (EM) spectrum. The actual detonation of the HARM warhead on the radar is a method of physical attack. Once the radar is destroyed, the SAM launch crew is denied the information required to acquire and track the friendly strike package, which thus makes it through to the target. |

**Figure 1.2. Examples of Physical, Electronic, and Information Attack**

command. To control is to regulate forces and functions to execute the commander's intent. C2 includes both the *process* by which the commander decides what action is to be taken and the *system* that

**directs and monitors the implementation of the decision.** Specifically, C2 includes the battlespace management process of planning, directing, coordinating, and controlling forces and operations. C2 involves the integration of systems, procedures, organizational structures, personnel, equipment, facilities, information, and communications designed to enable a commander to exercise command and control across the range of military operations. *Aerospace forces conduct command and control to meet strategic, operational, and tactical objectives.*

Air Force units are employed in a joint force context by a joint force commander. C2 of those forces can be through a Service component commander or a functional component commander if more than one Service's air assets are involved. This officer, the JFACC, should be the Service commander with the preponderance of air and space assets and the capability to plan, task, and control joint air and space operations. *It is a basic principle of aerospace doctrine that C2 of air and space forces be centralized under one officer—an airman.*

**The E-3A Sentry Airborne Warning and Control System (AWACS) provides a forward command and control node for the aerospace operations center (AOC) and greatly reduces the reaction time when countering time sensitive targets in the defensive counterair mission.**

## Airlift

**Airlift is the transportation of personnel and materiel through the air and can be applied across the entire range of military operations in support of national objectives.** Airlift provides rapid and flexible force-mobility options that allow military forces to respond to and operate in a wider variety of circumstances and time frames. A key function of the Air Force, airlift provides global reach for US military forces and the capability to quickly apply strategic global power to various crisis situations worldwide by delivering necessary forces. The power-projection capabilities that airlift supplies are vital since it provides the flexibility to get expeditionary forces to the point of a crisis with minimum delay. Accordingly, airlift is viewed as a foundation of US national security at the strategic level and as a crucial capability for operational and tactical commanders within a theater. *Therefore, airlift is not only a vital component of US defense policy but is critical to support overall national policy and objectives.*

Air Force airlift operations are typically classified as intertheater or intratheater. Operational Support Airlift (OSA) comprises a third and special classification of airlift operations. These operations are defined by the nature of the mission rather than the airframe used. Most aircraft are not exclusively assigned to one operational classification. In fact, the majority of the airlift force is capable of accomplishing any classification of airlift.

❂ **Intertheater airlift provides the airbridge that links theaters to the CONUS and to other theaters, as well as airlift within the CONUS.** Due to the global ranges usually involved, intertheater airlift is normally comprised of the heavy, intercontinental airlift assets, but may be augmented with shorter-range aircraft when required. Most of the forces responsible for executing intertheater airlift missions are under the operational control (OPCON) of the Commander, Air Mobility Command (AMC/CC).

❂ **Intratheater airlift provides the air movement of personnel and materiel within a geographic CINC's AOR.** Assets designated to provide intratheater airlift are either assigned or attached to that geographic CINC. This classification of airlift is generally fulfilled by aircraft capable of operation under a wide range of tactical conditions, including small, austere, unimproved airfield operations. Intratheater operations provide time-sensitive airlift to the commander, which may be critically needed to fulfill theater objectives.

✪ **Operational support airlift** is a special classification of operations providing for the timely movement of limited numbers of priority personnel and cargo during wartime as well as peacetime. OSA operations tend to be conducted by smaller-sized business type airframes. In most cases, these airframes are permanently assigned to a theater component or major air command (MAJCOM). While OSA operations are normally conducted in support of the assigned organization's organic requirements, OSA assets may be used to reduce extraordinary workload demands on the airlift system. United States Transportation Command (USTRANSCOM) is responsible for the scheduling and execution of OSA operations regarding CONUS based assets while the Services validate OSA requests.

### Air Refueling

**Air refueling is an integral part of US airpower across the range of military operations.** Air refueling, along with airlift, fulfills the Air Force contribution to the joint mobility role. It significantly expands the employment options available to a commander by increasing the range, endurance, payload, and flexibility of air forces. Therefore, aerial refueling is an essential capability in the conduct of air operations worldwide and is especially important when overseas basing is limited or not available. Air Force air refueling assets perform six basic missions: (1) Single Integrated Operation Plan (SIOP) support, (2) global attack support, (3) air bridge support, (4) deployment support, (5) theater support, and (6) special operations support.

**Air refueling provides additional options for the air strategist.** If forward locations are threatened, fighters and bombers may operate out of bases further to the rear for airbase security. The same option may work for cases where forward bases are unavailable for political or other reasons. A drawback to this option is increased mission duration, *which reduces the total number of sorties possible in a given period.*

### Spacelift

**Spacelift projects power by delivering satellites, payloads, and materiel into or through space.** During a period of increased tension or conflict, the spacelift objective is to launch or deploy new and replenishment space assets to achieve national security objectives. To satisfy this requirement, spacelift should be functional and flexible, capable of meeting the nation's full range of launch requirements from placing space systems in orbit. Equally important, spacelift should be timely and responsive to the user's needs. Air Force spacelift operations are conducted to either deploy, sustain, or augment satellite constellations supporting national security objectives.

○ **Launch to deploy** describes launches required to initially achieve a satellite system's designed operational capability. In this approach, space systems are launched on a predetermined schedule.

**Atlas II is the workhorse of the Air Force space launch program that evolved from the successful Atlas intercontinental ballistic missile (ICBM) program. It is designed to launch payloads into low earth orbit, transfer orbit, or geosynchronous orbit.**

○ **Launch to sustain** describes launches to replace satellites that are predicted to fail or abruptly fail. They may be scheduled well in advance or may require unscheduled operations.

○ **Launch to augment** describes launches to increase operational capability in response to contingency requirements, crisis, or war. Unscheduled launches or payload adjustment on scheduled activity will likely be required.

**Special Operations Employment**

Special operations employment is the use of special operations airpower, to conduct the following primary missions: unconventional warfare, direct action, special reconnaissance, combating terrorism, foreign internal defense, psychological operations (PSYOP), civil affairs, information operations, and counterproliferation. To execute special operations, Air Force special operations forces (AFSOF) are normally employed in small formations capable of both independent and supporting operations, with the purpose of enabling timely and tailored responses across the range of military operations.

AFSOF may accomplish tasks at the strategic, operational, or tactical levels of war or other contingency operations through the conduct of low-visibility, covert, or clandestine military actions. US Air Force special operations are usually conducted in enemy-controlled or politically sensitive territories and may complement or support conventional

**Air Force special operations aircraft perform infiltration of joint forces into hostile or denied areas.**

operations. AFSOF may be part of a joint special operations forces (SOF) team that provides combatant commanders with a synergistic capability to accomplish specialized tasks.

**Special operations differ from conventional operations in operational techniques, mode of employment, degree of covertness, independence from friendly support, and dependence on detailed operational intelligence and indigenous assets.** Those circumstances are often dominated by high risk and political, environmental, and operational constraints. In addition, governments often view the use of SOF as a means to control escalation in situations in which the use of conventional forces is unwarranted or undesirable. Accordingly, theater CINCs may choose to use special operations forces, working either independently or in support of conventional forces, to operate in rear areas to exploit enemy weaknesses or collect intelligence that would not otherwise be available. However, it should be emphasized that special operations forces can also operate as a strategic force independent of theater CINCs. Such employment should be carefully coordinated to prevent conflict with other operations.

**Intelligence, Surveillance, and Reconnaissance (ISR)**

**Intelligence provides clear, brief, relevant, and timely analysis on foreign capabilities and intentions for planning and conducting military operations.** *The overall objective of intelligence is to enable commanders and combat forces to "know the enemy."* It helps commanders across the range of military operations by collecting, analyzing, fusing, tailoring, and disseminating intelligence to the right place at the right time for key decision making. Intelligence provides indications of enemy intentions and guides decisions on how, when, and where to engage enemy forces to achieve the commander's objectives. It assists in combat assessment through munitions-effects assessment and bomb-damage assessment.

○ Intelligence organizations integrate technical and quantitative assessments with analytical judgments based on detailed knowledge of the way the enemy thinks and operates. Intelligence personnel should maintain an independent perspective. Commanders anticipate that even the best intelligence may not provide a complete picture, especially when the enemy is practicing deception or when the intelligence is derived from a single source. Still, intelligence gives commanders the best available estimate of enemy capabilities, COGs, and courses of action.

○ A useful tool for Air Force intelligence is *"intelligence preparation of the battlespace (IPB)."* IPB is a four-step systematic process of analyzing the threat and environment to help the commander better understand the many variables that can influence his mission and operations. The IPB methodology is an effective analytical process that can be used during peacetime, crisis, or at the tactical, operational, and strategic levels of war. While most of the individual actions that constitute IPB are nothing new to Air Force intelligence, establishing a consistent process will provide greater focus, thereby improving the overall effectiveness of aerospace power.

Specifically, IPB focuses on the relationship between the threat and environment, along with the effect of that interaction on both friendly and enemy courses of action. IPB results in the production of adversary courses of action, named areas of interest, and high-value targets, which are inputs to the JFACC/COMAFFOR campaign planning, intelligence collection, and targeting processes. When done properly, IPB facilitates getting "inside" the enemy's decision-making cycle. IPB is viewed by the US Air Force as a valuable methodology for focusing intelligence on the commander and the commanders' supporting C2 elements. Additional advantages include integrating analysis, collection management, and targeting processes, as well as providing a standardized analytic approach for training purposes. Air Force intelligence entities at all levels of command should use IPB principles, focusing on environmental and threat characteristics and activities that significantly influence air, space, and information operations. However, specific IPB products and procedures are left to the discretion of local commanders.

**Surveillance is the function of systematically observing air, space, surface, or subsurface areas, places, persons, or things, by visual, aural, electronic, photographic, or other means.** Surveillance is a continuing process, not oriented to a specific "target." In response to the requirements of military forces, surveillance must be designed to provide warning of enemy initiatives and threats and to detect changes in enemy activities. Airborne and space-based surveillance assets exploit elevation to detect enemy initiatives at long range. For example, its extreme elevation makes space-based missile-launch detection and tracking indispensable for defense against ballistic missile attack. Surveillance assets are now essential to national and theater defense and to the security of all military forces.

**Reconnaissance complements surveillance in obtaining, by visual observation or other detection methods, specific information about the activities and resources of an enemy or potential enemy; or in securing data concerning the meteorological, hydrographic, or geographic characteristics of a particular area.** Reconnaissance generally has a *time constraint* associated with the tasking. Collection capabilities including airborne and space-based systems, both manned and unmanned, and their associated support systems are tailored to provide the flexibility, responsiveness, versatility, and mobility required by the strenuous demands of fluid, global taskings. Intelligence critical to the prosecution of current combat operations is derived from reconnaissance operations and is evaluated and transmitted in near real time to those elements needing that information. *Intelligence, surveillance, and reconnaissance must operate together, enabling commanders to preserve forces, achieve economies, and accomplish campaign objectives.*

### Combat Search and Rescue (CSAR)

CSAR is an integral part of US combat operations and should be considered across the range of military operations. **CSAR consists of those air operations conducted to recover distressed personnel during wartime or contingency and is a key element in sustaining the morale, cohesion, and fighting capability of friendly forces.** It preserves critical combat resources and denies the enemy potential sources of intelligence. Although all US Air Force weapon systems have the

**Pararescuemen or "PJs" are a welcome sight to any downed aircrew member. Teamed with other CSAR forces, these highly trained and highly motivated airmen go directly into harm's way "so that others may live."**

inherent capability to support CSAR operations, the US Air Force maintains certain forces specifically dedicated for search, rescue, and recovery operations.

## Navigation and Positioning

**The function of navigation and positioning is to provide accurate location and time of reference in support of strategic, operational, and tactical operations.** Navigation and positioning help all military forces to precisely maneuver, synchronize actions, locate and attack targets, locate and recover downed aircrew, and other tasks requiring navigation and positioning accuracy. Navigation and positioning are key elements of information superiority and global awareness. Some key portions of navigation and positioning, such as the global positioning system (GPS) or ground-based navigation aides, may be exploited by the enemy. This should be taken into consideration when weighing the potential benefits versus potential threats of employing various systems.

## Weather Services

Weather services provided by the Air Force supply *timely and accurate environmental information, including both space environment and atmospheric weather,* to commanders for their objectives and plans at the strategic, operational, and tactical levels. They gather, analyze, and provide meteorological data for mission planning and execution. Environmental information is integral to the timing of operations, employment planning, and the conduct of air, ground, and space launch operations. *Weather services also influence the selection of targets, routes, weapon systems, and delivery tactics and are a key element of information superiority.*

## UNITY OF COMMAND

**Aerospace power best serves the nation's interests when tailored to operate across the entire region or theater of battle.** Doctrine supports this concept by first adhering to the fundamental principle of *unity of command.* One commander should have overall authority to

> *The very flexibility of air forces makes true cooperation essential. Air forces, at short notice, can be switched from one sort of target to another and, within limits, from one type of operation to a quite different type. There is, therefore, a constant temptation to use them piecemeal to meet an immediate requirement, rather than to use them on a long-term joint plan, and to utilize their flexibility in the method of achieving a consistent aim which is an integral part of our government's policy and our strategy to implement that policy.*
>
> **J.C. Slessor**
> **Air Marshall, Royal Air Force**

control all military operations within the theater. The JFC exploits the capabilities of his various forces to accomplish theater and strategic objectives. Similarly, aerospace power can be most effectively employed when led by a single airman, the JFACC, who is responsible for the planning and conduct of air warfare in a given operation or conflict. In order to benefit from unity of command, the JFACC follows principles that guide the organization, command and control, employment, and support for theater air forces.

### Joint Force Air Component Commander (JFACC)

**The JFACC is the professional airman with the requisite experience and expertise to integrate joint aerospace capabilities in meeting national and theater objectives.** In that capacity, the JFACC shares the JFC's vision on how to meet those objectives and translates the JFC's concept of operations into terms relevant to air and space missions. The

JFACC develops and executes an air operation to achieve the national and theater objectives for the JFC, as part of the overall theater campaign. *Essentially, the JFACC is the single airman responsible for planning and directing joint aerospace operations to maximize overall combat power for the JFC.*

### JFACC Designation

**Theater air commanders (JFACCs) devise ways to exploit the different capabilities of the available air and space assets while reducing their limitations; they also plan operations that help maximize the combat power of both the aerospace and surface efforts, and consequently conduct an effective theater air campaign.** Operation DESERT STORM provided a modern combat validation of the JFACC concept, reinforced during operations in Bosnia and Kosovo, that demonstrated the effectiveness of centralizing C2 of aerospace power. Current joint doctrine acknowledges the lessons of history by recommending that JFCs normally designate a JFACC to ensure the proper application of the aerospace effort within a theater of operations. Normally, the component commander with the preponderance of air and space assets and the capability to plan, task, and control joint aerospace operations is designated as the JFACC. This individual should have comprehensive knowledge and understanding of aerospace power doctrine and be trained in the application of aerospace power to achieve strategic, operational, and tactical objectives. Under most circumstances the commander of Air Force forces is designated the JFACC, and as such will be the supported commander for aerospace operations that are within or affect the theater of operations.

### JFACC Responsibilities and Authority

**The essence of the JFACC concept is the unified development of a concept of air operations supporting the joint campaign plan to meet the JFC's objectives.** JFCs define the JFACC's responsibilities and authority based on these objectives. The individual designated as the JFACC uses established procedures with the joint force headquarters and the other components to fulfill JFC-assigned tasks. These include planning, coordinating, tasking, and directing the overall aerospace effort, and recommending apportionment of aerospace power to the JFC. The JFACC is normally the area air defense commander (AADC) and the airspace control authority (ACA). The JFC establishes the specific command authority for the JFACC to accomplish those responsibilities. The JFACC typically exercises OPCON over assigned and attached forces and tactical control (TACON) over other military capabilities and forces made available for tasking. Certain aerospace forces, such as intertheater airlift and space assets, may not come under the operational control of the JFACC but will still support operations. Some air assets, such as the Army Tactical Missile System (ATACMS), Tomahawk land-attack missiles (TLAMs), SOF aircraft, and Army/Marine attack helicopters, might remain under the OPCON of the respective component commanders. Normally, the JFACC needs only TACON or an established supported/supporting relationship to conduct operations with augmenting forces that remain assigned to other components. For example, the JFACC is normally designated the *supported commander* for counterair operations. When aerospace operations constitute the bulk of the capability needed to directly attack strategic COGs, JFCs will normally task the JFACC, as a supported commander, to conduct such operations. The JFACC will also designate targets or objectives for other components in support of the joint strategic attack effort. The JFACC is also the supported commander for joint air interdiction and will use JFC priorities to plan and execute the theaterwide interdiction effort. *It is important to recognize that the JFACC retains a theaterwide focus, and joint doctrine specifies the use of smaller areas of operations (AOs) only for surface forces.*

## JOINT FORCE AIR ASSETS

**The primary purpose for designating a JFACC is to provide unity of the aerospace effort for the benefit of the joint force as a whole.** Component commanders make air and space capabilities/forces available to the JFC for tasking to support the joint force as a whole based on the JFC's mission. Normally, these capabilities/forces are provided by the JFC to the JFACC for tasking.

✪ The **US Navy** retains organic control of those assets required for fleet defense and related naval missions. TLAM and fixed-wing sorties in excess of those needed to satisfy maritime air operations requirements are normally made available to the JFACC.

✪ **Army aviation** assets are normally retained for employment as organic forces. However, some Army helicopters can be employed for AI or SEAD, in which case they come under the purview of the JFACC. The same holds true for other systems (such as ATACMs) when employed for AI or SEAD, depending on tasking and target location.

**US Army AH-64 Apache helicopters firing tube launched, optically tracked, wire guided (TOW) missiles made the first attacks against Iraqi ground radar sites, clearing a path for penetrating air attacks during the opening moments of the Gulf War.**

✪ **For Marine aviation assets,** the Marine air-ground task force (MAGTF) commander normally retains operational control of organic air assets. Because the US Marine Corps' surface forces do not bring a large amount of heavy artillery to the battle, their need for CAS is greater than most Army units. As a result, CAS is considered an essential component of Marine battlefield firepower. During joint operations, the MAGTF makes sorties available to the JFC, for tasking through the JFACC for air defense, interdiction, and reconnaissance. In addition to those requirements, those sorties in excess of MAGTF direct support requirements are provided to the JFC for tasking through the JFACC for support of other joint force components or the joint force as a whole.

✪ **The joint force special operations component commander (JFSOCC),** when established, exercises operational control over all theater assigned joint special operations forces that have been made available for tasking by the Services. The Joint Special Operations Air Component Commander (JSOACC) would then control all theater assigned special operations aviation assets. The JSOACC centralizes control of special operations aviation much as the JFACC does for conventional airpower. Alternatively, Air Force special operations forces may be placed under the OPCON or TACON of the COMAFFOR or JFACC.

## EXAMPLES OF AIR WARFARE

Air power can be employed in as many different ways as there are different kinds of warfare. Nevertheless, there are certain doctrinal concepts, such as the tenets of airpower, that apply at least generally to most cases. The following are examples of US Air Force doctrine on aerospace force employment in several different types of warfare. Not all functions are illustrated in every example; some, like ISR and C2, are assumed to be employed in all scenarios. The intent is to show how the role of some functions change as a campaign develops.

### Guerrilla Warfare

Guerrilla warfare is defined in joint doctrine as *"military and paramilitary operations conducted in enemy-held or hostile territory by irregular, predominantly indigenous forces."* While sometimes limited enough to qualify as a military operations other than war (MOOTW), guerrilla warfare can also be considered true warfare when the level of violence is high enough. This was the case for operations in South Vietnam during the Vietnam War, to cite one example. Aerospace power can be used effectively in guerrilla warfare but will often be employed in either a supporting role or some other form of operation that differs from the conventional application of force against "traditional" targets. A guerrilla enemy is typically equipped with light weapons, often of relatively low technology. Air superiority will not normally be challenged; enemy air defense weapons often consist solely of light antiaircraft guns and shoulder-launched SAMs. On the other hand, the enemy may enjoy support in the local populace, and disrupting the enemy's support base through physical means may prove difficult. Although the level of information sophistication of the enemy may vary greatly from one region to another, it is becoming increasingly easy for small units in remote locations to access data worldwide.

As with all military operations, aerospace power success in guerrilla warfare requires a thorough understanding of the military and national objectives and strategy. The character and scope of aerospace operations will directly depend on the objectives they support. Under some circumstances, airlift may represent the bulk of the air component's contribution to the war effort, providing mobility and resupply to ground forces operating in remote areas. Special forces airpower may play a large role in guerrilla warfare, especially for counterinsurgency operations. IO such as PSYOP and ISR are uses of aerospace forces that may also play a critical role in guerrilla warfare.

Figure 1.3 illustrates one possible scenario, in which only a small portion of the available air and space assets are required for *air superiority,* and a large percentage of that is directed against surface-to-air targets. *ISR* remains a vital part of the operation from beginning to end, as gaining intelligence on enemy movements can be very difficult under guerrilla warfare conditions. *PSYOP* is important and is used to win the local populace over through keeping them informed of actual events as they transpire. This use of IO to overcome adversary propaganda is a vital part of the campaign. *Air mobility* is also a key use of air assets, both in support of actual combat operations and in resupply of remote ground forces that enable monitoring of the entire country. *Counterland* attacks are often made when enemy forces concentrate for conventional attacks, since they become vulnerable when massing for attack or operating in the open as conventional ground combat formations. Except for these occasional counterland attacks, there is not a large need for conventional force application since lucrative targets for air attack do not exist.

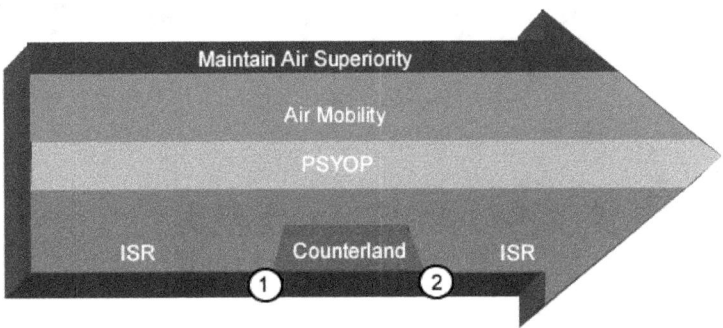

Note: At phase point 1, a lucrative target for counterland attack is identified and attacked. At point 2, this target has been neutralized and counterland operations cease.

**Figure 1.3. Sample Use of Airpower During Guerrilla Warfare**

## Forced Entry

Forced entry operations are typically short in duration but may involve high levels of conventional combat. Friendly ground forces are inserted via various delivery methods to accomplish ground objectives, while aerospace power operates in various supported and supporting roles. The actual functions and missions performed vary with specific circumstances; for example, aerospace power might play a greater role during an airborne force insertion than during an amphibious operation. Operation JUST CAUSE in Panama was an example of forced entry warfare that relied heavily on aerospace forces for both mobility and force application. There may be a need to devote a large force to aerospace superiority, since forced entry operations are usually planned for short duration and there may not be time for a protracted aerospace superiority campaign. Surface forces may be employed in very vulnerable modes of insertion, so enemy air and missile reaction must be reduced to minimum levels. Forced entry operations may take place at long distances from friendly bases, so the judicious use of both air refueling and naval aviation assets is important.

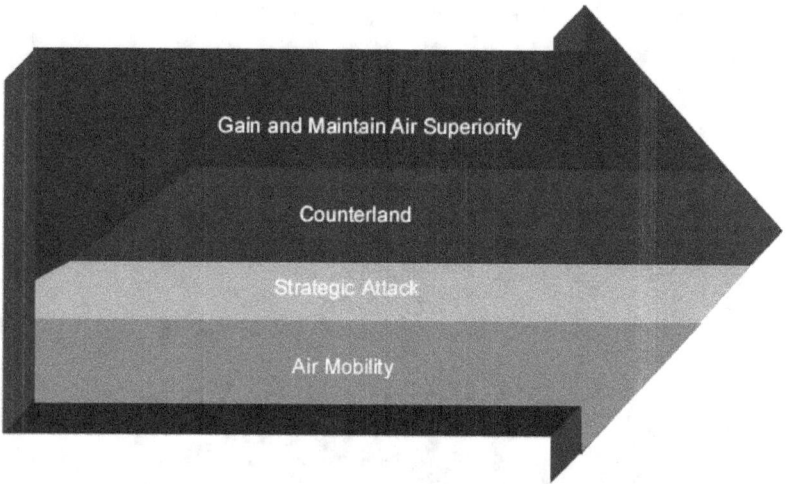

Note: This example shows the large initial use of counterair and air mobility, with some strategic attack performed by forces capable of penetrating high-threat air defense networks (stealth and cruise missile assets). As air superiority is achieved, counterland operations begin.

**Figure 1.4. Sample Use of Airpower for Forced Entry Campaigns**

Figure 1.4 illustrates the use of aerospace forces in a sample airborne forced entry operation. The key functions performed early on are aerospace superiority and air mobility, since the enemy threat must be eliminated and the friendly force must be delivered to the surface area of operations. Once in place, and once the enemy aerospace threat is neutralized, counterland operations ramp up to both destroy the enemy ground force reserves and support the engaged friendly ground units. Some strategic attack is also employed, mainly against enemy C2 centers that will have immediate effects on the battlefield. Due to the short duration of the operation, other strategic attacks that would have longer-delayed effects are not employed.

**Decisive Halt**

A decisive halt operation is employed to stop an advancing enemy ground force prior to reaching its objective, which typically is to seize and occupy a certain amount of territory. Aerospace forces provide an unmatched global response capability to perform decisive halt, and often represent the only force application available on short notice to perform expeditionary tasks. When a decisive halt is performed during conventional warfare, the enemy will often have a robust air defense system and may possess a significant offensive aerospace capability of their own. This requires a large application of counterair force early on, which can ramp down to a maintenance level as the conflict progresses. As with forced entry, the timespace of a decisive halt may be limited (the enemy must be stopped before they have time to reach their objectives). This will mandate the use of counterland in more of a direct attack mode than in longer scenarios, and strategic attack should be restricted to those targets whose payoff will be realized in the time allowed. There may not be any need for traditional CAS, as the bulk of friendly ground forces may not arrive in theater until after the halt has been accomplished.

Figure 1.5 shows one possible decisive halt scenario, which starts with long-range strikes on counterair targets and some key strategic targets. Depending on availability of nearby airbases, in-place forces and aircraft carriers, the bulk of the first few days' attacks may come from global-reach missions launched from bases outside the theater. This places a heavy demand on air refueling assets, which will also be heavily tasked to support the deployment of shorter range air assets and ground forces into the theater. Counterland attacks, primarily air interdiction of the invading enemy ground force, grow to become the bulk of missions flown until the halt is achieved. This illustration is similar to that for the forced entry

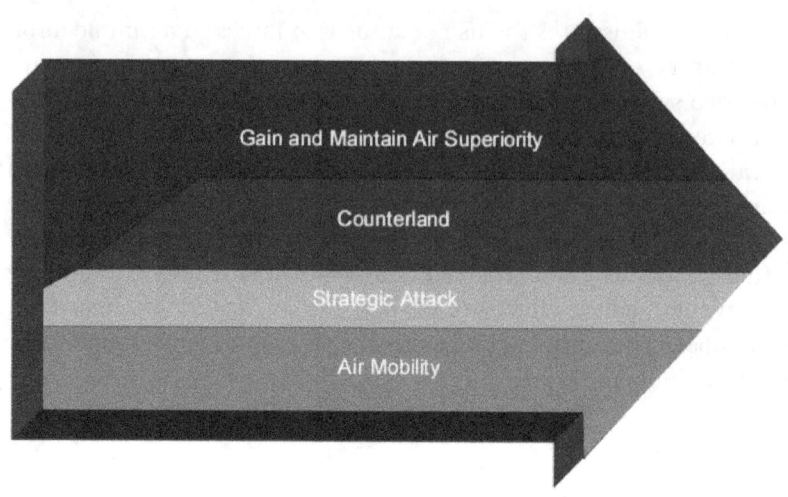

**Figure 1.5. Sample Use of Airpower for Decisive Halt**

example, with the exception that the air mobility effort to bring ground forces into theater may be smaller (or possibly not required). This is especially true if the allied nation involved can provide a capable, on-scene ground combat force.

### Global Conflict

The cold war era was an example of global conflict that was deterred from ever reaching its full destructive potential, with only occasional outbreaks of combat between the superpowers or their allies. Nuclear weapons, along with other weapons of mass destruction (WMD), have such devastating potential that deterrence, not combat, has fortunately remained their primary use. As the United States develops its strategy for the post-cold war era, the global reach mission has become a province of conventional forces. The US Air Force is becoming more expeditionary in nature, with fewer forces permanently stationed at overseas locations from which force may be directly applied against an enemy. The AEF provides a task-oriented force that can be rapidly deployed to any part of the globe, to perform any of the lethal or nonlethal missions assigned to the Air Force. Naval airpower can supplement the AEF, depending on the proximity of the theater to accessible sea approaches.

Global power missions, such as B-52 and B-2 strikes from CONUS bases, provide an important source of aerospace power that does not depend on either forward bases or sea access, although long-range missions result in far fewer sorties per day than in-theater forces can provide. This is somewhat offset by the large number of weapons that can be carried by long-range bombers and a growing family of independently targetable precision weapons that enable strikes against multiple targets during a single bomber sortie. Shorter-range forces can also be employed on very long-range missions, provided proper air refueling support is available. An example of this was the Libyan raid of 1986 using multiple refuelings to support fighter attacks at intercontinental ranges. All of the examples listed in this section employ some degree of the Air Force's global reach capability; the amount they actually use depends on numerous factors that range from geographic distance to political support from allied and neutral nations.

# CHAPTER TWO

# AIR WARFARE PLANNING

*Air power can win battles, or it can win wars.*

**General William Momyer**

Campaign plans provide practical guidance for the employment of forces at the operational level of war. In a major conflict, a campaign may be one of a series of campaigns needed to support a strategy that accomplishes national objectives. Campaigns tie military strategy and objectives to the battlespace. Just as a conductor directs the timing, tempo, and phasing for an orchestra, so too the campaign plan directs the conduct of tactical operations to achieve strategic goals.

## OVERALL JOINT PLANNING

Joint planning is normally conducted via the *deliberate planning process,* which produces operations plans (OPLANs) as the end product. OPLANs provide detailed guidance, including deployment and logistical support, for areas of the world where possible conflict may occur at some future time. *Crisis action planning,* on the other hand, occurs in response to an actual contingency and produces as its output an OPORD that is, if needed, executed by the National Command Authorities (NCA) to put military forces into motion. Figure 2.1 compares the two planning procedures.

**Simply stated, an OPLAN serves as the key employment concept of the theater of war and theater of operations.** It is the basis for all other planning among the staff and various subordinate commands. It provides the joint commander's vision and intent through broad concepts for operations and sustainment for the duration of the situation. For large multiphase conflicts, a campaign plan with supporting OPLANs might be developed. Regardless of which type of process is used, the resulting plan provides strategic military objectives and operational direction. A distinction is made for each phase of the conflict, and an end state for each should be clearly defined. Reorganization of forces or resources may be required at the end of a phase before another action is initiated. The plan organizes and tasks subordinate forces. It furthermore designates command relationships, additional responsibilities, and objectives.

| | Crisis Action Planning | Deliberate Planning |
|---|---|---|
| Time Available to Plan | Hours or Days | 18 24 Months |
| Joint Planning and Execution Community (JPEC) Involvement | For security reasons, possibly very limited using close hold procedures | Participates fully |
| Phases | 6 phases from situation development to execution | 5 phases from initiation to supporting plans |
| Document Assigning Tasks | WARNING ORDER to CINC; CINC assigns tasks with EVALUATION REQUEST message | Joint Strategic Capabilities Plan (JSCP) to CINC; CINC assigns tasks with planning or other written directive |
| Forces for Planning | **ALLOCATED** in the WARN ING, PLANNING, ALERT, or EXECUTE ORDER | APPORTIONED in JSCP |
| Early Planning Guidance to Staff | WARNING ORDER from CJCS; CINC's EVALUATION REQUEST | Planning Directive issued by CINC after planning guidance step of concept development phase |
| Commander's Estimate | Communicates recommendations of CINC to the CJCS/NCA | Communicates the CINC's DECISION to staff and subordinate commanders |
| Decision on Course of Action (COA) | NCA decide COA | CINC decides COA with review by CJCS |
| Execution Document | EXECUTE ORDER | |
| Products | Campaign plan (If required) with supporting OPORDs, or OPORD with supporting OPORDs | OPLAN, CONPLAN or FUNCTIONAL PLAN with supporting plans |

Reference: Joint Pub 5-03.1 (to be published as CJCSM 3122.01), JOPES Volume I

Figure 2.1. Comparing Crisis Action Planning Procedures With Deliberate Planning Procedures

JAOP ensures synchronization and integration of aerospace, land, maritime, information, and special operations efforts into a synergistic whole.

**Planning such operations revolves around precise communication of commander's intent and a shared, clear understanding of the appropriate operational concepts at each level of command.** Once the overall strategy has been formulated for fighting the war, the theater commander imparts it to his component commanders. They then devise a game plan for supporting the national strategy by integrating the assets under their command. It is from this point onward that strategic concepts are translated into operational missions. The JFC's strategic appreciation and articulation of the strategic and operational objectives needed to accomplish the mission form the basis for determining the component objectives. The capabilities of aerospace power, whether acting as the decisive force or in support of other components, must be included in strategic planning at the highest level. *If the JFC focuses solely on the classic "post-buildup counterattack" as the decisive phase of combat, he may miss an opportunity to drive the enemy out of the fight early on with aerospace power.*

✪ **Campaign plans set long-term goals** such as control of a geographic area or the defeat of an enemy in the theater of operations. Accordingly, campaign plans normally provide both a general plan for the entire campaign and specific plans for the campaign's various phases.

✪ **The JFC should specify how to defeat the enemy.** This plan also aims for the fastest possible solution at the lowest possible cost in lives and materiel. A protracted campaign rarely serves strategic purposes well and usually increases friendly force exposure to losses.

✪ **Above all, the method selected should be effective and militarily achievable.** An effective campaign plan focuses on the enemy's vulnerable COGs—those military, political, economic, or informational points from which an adversary derives its freedom of action, physical strength, or will to fight. If such a COG is attacked (or merely threatened), the enemy's position may become untenable.

In order for aerospace options to be properly planned, presented, the theater commander should have a representative number of airmen in the key positions on the joint staff. This is particularly important if the JFC is not an airman. Especially during crisis action planning, the JFACC and the airmen on the CINC's joint staff should ensure that *all possible aerospace options are examined in the formulation of overall joint courses of action.*

## THE JOINT AIR OPERATIONS PLAN (JAOP)

Normally, the JFACC has the responsibility of developing the JAOP in support of the JFC's overall theater plan. The JFACC provides the JFC the means to exploit joint aerospace capabilities, and the JAOP is the vehicle through which the JFACC directs joint aerospace power. The JFACC plans and conducts operations in coordination with the other component commanders, creating a unified effort to accomplish theater military objectives. While the JFACC provides the central guidance for conduct of the theater air campaign, the JFC sequences and resolves component requirements and priorities. *The JAOP provides the blueprint for air and space tasking, which will be implemented through the daily air tasking order (ATO) process.* The ATO is typically not developed until operations actually commence, but some contingency plans include an "on-the-shelf" air tasking order for the first few days of a possible conflict.

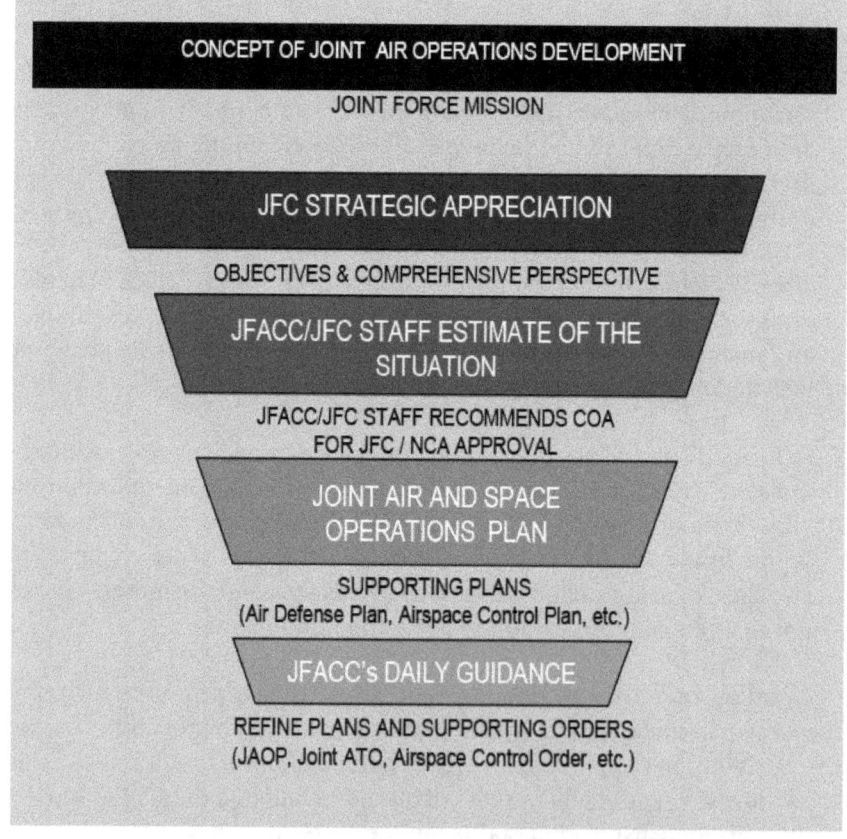

**Figure 2.2. Joint Air Operations Development**

The JFACC uses the JFC's strategic and operational objectives to develop an air estimate of the situation that results in the formulation of a course of action (COA). Once the air commander's COA is approved by the JFC, it becomes the basic concept for joint air operations, stating what is to be accomplished. The JAOP and supporting plans state how the air component commander will conduct aerospace operations. *This is the heart of what is colloquially called "the air campaign."*

## PLANNING JOINT AIR OPERATIONS

In developing the JAOP, the JFACC leverages combinations of forces and actions to achieve the assigned objective(s) in the shortest time and with minimal casualties. The JFACC arranges symmetric and asymmetric actions to take advantage of friendly strengths and enemy vulnerabilities; this also preserves freedom of action for future operations. *Where possible, COGs are targeted to provide the greatest effect for the force employed.*

### JAOP Planning Process

Normally, there are five stages in the joint air operations planning process, and each stage produces a desired product. While presented in a sequential order, the steps are not all required to be completed in the given order. Work on the various phases may be concurrent or sequential. At some point, however, the stages must be integrated and the products of each phase must be checked and verified for consistency.

✪ **Operational Environment Research.** The product of this phase is primarily the *intelligence preparation of the battlespace* that presents an in-depth knowledge of the operational environment. This phase is focused on gaining information about friendly and adversary capabilities and intentions, doctrine, and the environment in which the operations will take place. The goal of this phase is to gain an understanding of the theater of operations, the adversary, and friendly forces available to accomplish the JFC's objectives. Key factors such as threats and airbase availability will affect the strategy development process. A larger enemy air threat requires more time and assets dedicated to the achievement of air superiority, to the initial detriment of other missions. Airfields further from the AOR may be used by long-range or tanker-assisted assets, but the increased mission duration will reduce the number of targets that can be attacked in a given period.

Such airfields may be at lower risk to enemy air and missile attack, however, providing a tradeoff between efficiency and survivability.

✪ **Objective Determination.** The products of this phase are *clearly defined and quantifiable objectives* that will contribute to the accomplishment of the JFC's overall objectives.

> ✪✪ The source of planning objectives is usually documented in the JFC's initial planning guidance and the operation or campaign plan.

> ✪✪ Joint air objectives are derived from the JFC's objectives.

> ✪✪ Aerospace power can impact all three levels of war and can perform independent, integrated, and supporting operations sequentially or simultaneously.

> ✪✪ Joint air objectives and supporting objectives should be identified by listing those objectives at each level of war. The objectives of each level should support the objectives of the next higher level to ensure unity of effort.

✪ **Centers of Gravity Identification.** The product of this phase is the identification of those strategic, operational, and tactical COGs whose destruction or disruption will achieve JFACC and JFC objectives. Clausewitz described a COG as "the hub of all power and movement, on which everything depends." Joint doctrine defines COGs as "those characteristics, capabilities, or localities from which a military force, nation, or alliance derives its freedom of action, physical strength, or will to fight." A COG describes the central features of an enemy system's or force's power that, if defeated, may have the most decisive result. Aerospace power typically has the ability to attack COGs throughout the AOR/joint operations area (JOA). It is important to remember that the type of COG and method of attack may vary widely throughout the range of military operations. Attacks may be restricted by political considerations, military risk, laws of armed conflict (LOAC), and rules of engagement (ROE). Examples of pertinent questions to consider when selecting a potential COG include: Will disruption of activity at this target satisfy a military objective? Is aerospace power the most appropriate and efficient way to strike this target? Are the expected results commensurate with the military risk? Proper analysis of what constitutes a COG, and how best to attack it, form the heart of this phase in JAOP planning.

○ **Strategy Identification.** The product of this phase is a *clearly defined joint aerospace strategy statement.* The operation or campaign plan communicates the JFC's strategy. The joint aerospace strategy states how the JFACC plans to exploit joint air and space capabilities and forces to support the JFC's objectives. While designed to maximize the efficient use of aerospace power, strategy should balance efficiency against competing factors such as political restraints, ROE, and the time available for effects to be felt by the enemy. *Aerospace strategy is not developed in a vacuum but is closely integrated with the other Services' planning efforts to support the overall strategy.*

○ **JAOP Development.** The product of this phase is the final joint air operations plan that details how joint aerospace employment will support the JFC's operation or campaign plan. Based on the JFC's guidance, the JFACC develops the JAOP. The joint air operations plan developed during this process should:

✪✪ Integrate the efforts of joint air capabilities and forces in achieving JFC objectives.

✪✪ Identify objectives and targets by priority order, describing in what order they should be attacked or dealt with, the desired results, and the weight of effort required to achieve the desired results in support of the JFC's objectives.

✪✪ Account for current and potential adversary offensive and defensive threats.

✪✪ Indicate the phasing of joint air operations in relation to the JFC's operation or campaign plan.

## Phasing

**Phasing provides an orderly schedule of military decisions and indicates preplanned shifts in priorities and intent.** The joint air operation can consist of several phases, with priority given to operations that can achieve theater-level objectives. The JFACC uses varying combinations of the functions and missions of aerospace power to accomplish the objectives in each phase. The following factors influence the decisions on phasing the JAOP:

✪ **Methods of Phasing. Phasing is accomplished in a variety of ways.** In cases when the JFC establishes phasing, this is the starting point for determining JAOP phasing. A few of the more common methods for phasing are by region, objectives, or force limitations. Commanders or planners should clearly identify start points, phase objectives, and measures of merit which define when the phase is complete. Note that the end point of one phase does not have to be the start point on the next phase. Phases will usually overlap to some extent and may occur simultaneously. Phasing guidance should identify phase objectives, tasks, and priorities.

✪ **Prioritization of Attack.** The JFC may prioritize theater military objectives, which the JFACC uses to orient the JAOP to meet JFC priorities. A conscious decision to prioritize objectives can drive the phasing of the JAOP by dictating a specific mission flow. This is based on strategic and operational considerations and translates into assignment of relative values for specific target sets and individual targets. The JFACC directs attacks on the selected target sets in parallel, series, or some combination of the two. *Attack in series* generally refers to attacking targets in the highest priority target set sequentially, beginning with the highest priority target and continuing to the lowest priority, before initiating attack on the next target set. *Parallel attack* refers to multiple, simultaneous attacks against targets with different priority levels. This is usually the preferred method, as it generates greater disruption and shock effects on the enemy. Because of airpower's flexibility and the technologies of precision and stealth, air forces are becoming more able to conduct parallel warfare. Parallel warfare uses aerospace power to attack key enemy systems and forces in order to paralyze its ability to function as it desires. Parallel warfare can use simultaneous attacks in time, space, and at all levels of war to control the enemy's functions and activities. *If the enemy's key targets, target sets, or COGs can be found and identified, they are usually within airpower's reach.* This presents the enemy leadership (military and political) with the dilemma of trying to cope with multiple threats against multiple possible targets.

✪ **Battlespace Control.** JFCs normally seek aerospace and information superiority early in the conduct of operations. Establishing control of aerospace is normally the key objective in the first phase of the JAOP. In general, aerospace control is a prerequisite to effective pursuit of other objectives.

Not every operation requires phasing. *Because of the unique nature and capabilities of aerospace power, it may be artificially constraining for the JFACC to describe the air campaign in terms of linear phases.* Phasing is a tool used by theater commanders to achieve synchronization in time. Air operations usually occur simultaneously and are considered complete when the desired effect is achieved, not after a given time or when a specific geographic point is reached. However, phasing can be a useful tool to communicate the JFACC's concept of operations.

**Once friendly forces can operate without unacceptable risk from enemy attack, aerospace operations often focus on neutralizing the enemy COGs.** The goal is to apply force against those points whose disruption will achieve maximum effect in support of aerospace objectives and corresponding theater objectives. Air interdiction can also significantly affect the course of a campaign. It contributes by interfering with the enemy's ability to command, mass, maneuver, withdraw, supply, and reinforce available combat power and by weakening the enemy physically and psychologically. It also creates opportunities for friendly commanders to exploit. The task of CAS is to provide selective and discriminate firepower, when and where needed, in support of land forces. It provides the land commander with highly mobile, responsive, and concentrated firepower; enhances the element of surprise; can employ munitions with great precision; and can attack targets that are inaccessible or invulnerable to surface fire. Although CAS is the least efficient application of air forces, at times it may be their most critical mission, particularly when it is required to exploit the success or ensure the survival of ground forces.

Measures of Success

**Measures of success, or indicators, are required to determine whether or not individual air and space missions, phases of an air campaign, or an air campaign in general are meeting objectives.** Assessment of such indicators should take place at the operational and even strategic levels of war and goes beyond counting craters or vehicles destroyed. The key is to determine when the predetermined conditions have been met that affect enemy operational employment or overall strategy. Continuing intelligence analysis helps to ensure that proper measurements take place.

Some attention should be paid to the specific process of how to determine measures of success. When possible, measures should not relate directly to tactical actions but to higher level objectives. For example, the first phase of an air campaign is often the achievement of some required level of aerospace superiority. An obviously poor measure would simply be to count friendly OCA sorties flown (although simple sortie counting has been used in past conflicts). A better measure might be of *enemy* sorties flown, since this relates more directly to the denial of aerospace use by the enemy. An even better measure would take other factors into account, such as human intelligence (HUMINT) and imagery intelligence (IMINT) of enemy air and missile capability, readiness, morale, and other factors. The downside of a more complete measure is that it becomes difficult to quantify, and therefore more subjective to personal interpretation. As with many things, the best measures are probably those that are a compromise between objective and subjective specifics, taken with a proper understanding of the limitations involved. *Measures that are used to indicate the completion of one phase in a campaign are especially important, as are those that could require a possible need to change the applied strategy.*

### JAOP Planning Factors

The following are some critical factors to consider in developing the joint air operations plan:

❂ **The Enemy's Strategy.** Sun Tzu's advice to defeat the enemy's strategy is as applicable today as it was over 2,500 years ago. This entails not only understanding the nature of the enemy, but also the enemy's specific objectives and willingness to sacrifice to achieve those objectives. An enemy may be described as rational, irrational, fanatic, rigid, flexible, independent, innovative, determined, doctrinaire, or countless other ways. Knowledge of the extent to which an enemy fits one of these categories can assist in determining the enemy's plans and how they will react to a new situation. *Therefore, the JFACC uses a broad range of national, theater, and tactical intelligence capabilities to effectively assess the enemy's strategy in order to defeat it. In this effort, the JFACC should guard against being too reactive when planning strategy.*

❂ **Logistics.** Military power achieves its full potential when operations and logistics harmonize to maximize mission effectiveness. Logistics considerations are a key factor in sequencing and sustaining forces and should be integral to the planning process. An air campaign's reach cannot exceed logistics' ability to support it. The JAOP should allocate sufficient forces of whatever type required to protect all aspects of the logistics network: embarkation, transportation, debarkation, distribution, and logistics information systems.

✪ **Air Mobility. Air mobility** is a key part of any JAOP. *Air refueling* is normally required for any large-scale deployment or employment of air assets and may often be the determining factor of how much aerospace power can be applied during a given period. *Air mobility* plays a vital role in deploying both aerospace and surface forces to an expeditionary location and can be considered part of force application when delivering airborne assets directly into battle via airdrop. Air mobility is also key to the sustainment of extended combat operations; JAOP planners should anticipate the need for continued delivery of fuel, ammunition, replacement parts, and all of the other items that are required for modern warfare. Proper synchronization of both intratheater and intertheater airlift with other aerospace operations is therefore required. In the case of intertheater airlift, there may be other taskings outside the combat theater that place some demand on the available airlift.

✪ **Space.** Operations DESERT STORM, DELIBERATE FORCE, AND ALLIED FORCE highlighted the increasing role space systems and forces have in planning and conducting theater air operations. Space assets (reconnaissance, surveillance, navigation, weather, and communications systems) are a primary means of collecting and transmitting information for intelligence preparation of the battlespace. These systems play an equally important role supporting the JFACC, in concert with Commander in Chief, US Space Command (USCINCSPACE), to assess the enemy's space capabilities and determine the impact they might have on the theater air campaign. Space plays an especially vital role in providing secure, survivable communications, both inter- and intratheater, to the communications dependent JFACC staff. Additionally, US Air Force space support teams augment the JFACC staff to provide in-depth space expertise in support of the planning and execution of air and space missions. For example, ballistic missile warning enhances the JFACC's counterair operations when conducting theater ballistic missile defense. *The increasing role of space in warfighting, and the similarity of the effects it produces to those produced by air-breathing assets, has led to the concept of a single aerospace medium when discussing military applications.*

# TOOLS FOR JOINT AIR OPERATIONS PLANNING

## Strategic Appreciation

Intelligence analysis supports the *strategic appreciation,* which forms a key foundation for the joint air campaign plan. A process that guides intelligence analysis is *intelligence preparation of the battlespace.* In developing the strategic appreciation, the JFC needs assessments of enemy forces concerning strength, capabilities, availability, sustainability, composition, disposition, movement of forces and weapon systems, leadership, transportation, energy, and information infrastructure.

The strategic appreciation is an evaluation of the political, economic, military, and social environments affecting the theater. It is one of the most useful products of the initial planning stage and is developed using a five-step process that can help clarify the nature of the conflict. The five steps are:

✪ Assess the strategic context of the conflict.

✪ Analyze enemy and friendly objectives.

✪ Explicitly state campaign assumptions.

✪ Compare friendly and enemy capabilities and limitations.

✪ Assess costs to both sides.

The goal is to understand the potential conflict and to conduct military planning with a sound appreciation of social, political, and economic considerations. This process is applicable across the range of military operations. The strategic appreciation can help to identify potential enemy and friendly COGs early in planning. Details of the strategic appreciation are found in Appendix A.

## Air Estimate of the Situation

The strategic appreciation is used by the JFACC to devise the *air estimate of the situation.* This estimate helps identify enemy COGs to attack and friendly COGs to defend. It follows a logical process to establish a sound course of action. The JFACC produces an estimate at the request of the JFC, or the JFACC and joint air operations center (JAOC) staff may develop one at an appropriate planning stage. The "estimate of the situation" uses a systematic approach to propose courses of action for solving a military problem. The air estimate may become part of the overall CINC's estimate, used to present possible courses of action to the NCA. There are five key steps to writing the estimate, which are briefly described in Appendix B.

✪ State the overall theater objectives.

✪ Develop friendly COAs.

✪ Analyze opposing COAs.

✪ Compare friendly and enemy COAs.

✪ Recommend friendly COA to JFC.

**JAOP Format**

**The joint air operations plan uses the same format as the JFC campaign plan but from an aerospace point of view.** Each JAOP differs with the AOR/JOA, situation, and capabilities of the joint force; a sample JAOP format is included in Appendix C. Various other informal tools and models for the aerospace planner are listed in Appendix G.

# CHAPTER THREE

# EXECUTING AIR WARFARE

Once the JAOP and its guidance have been developed, the operational art of aerospace planning prior to execution of operations is essentially finished. *When operations begin, an air tasking cycle is normally established to develop daily tactical tasking (the ATO) based on the operational guidance provided by the JAOP and other inputs.* It provides for the efficient and effective employment of the air and space assets of one or more components. The air tasking cycle is an interrelated series of actions that begins with the JFC's guidance for the cycle period. The JFACC's joint air operations center staff then develops a plan to support that guidance and develops an apportionment recommendation for the JFC to execute the plan. Finally, the JFACC allocates resources based on the JFC's apportionment decision and publishes the ATO. The ATO, when combined with the airspace control order (ACO) and special instructions (SPINS), provides operational and tactical direction for air operations throughout the range of military operations, as well as requesting the appropriate support from space assets not under the OPCON of the JFACC. The ATO is subsequently implemented by the theater air control system (TACS).

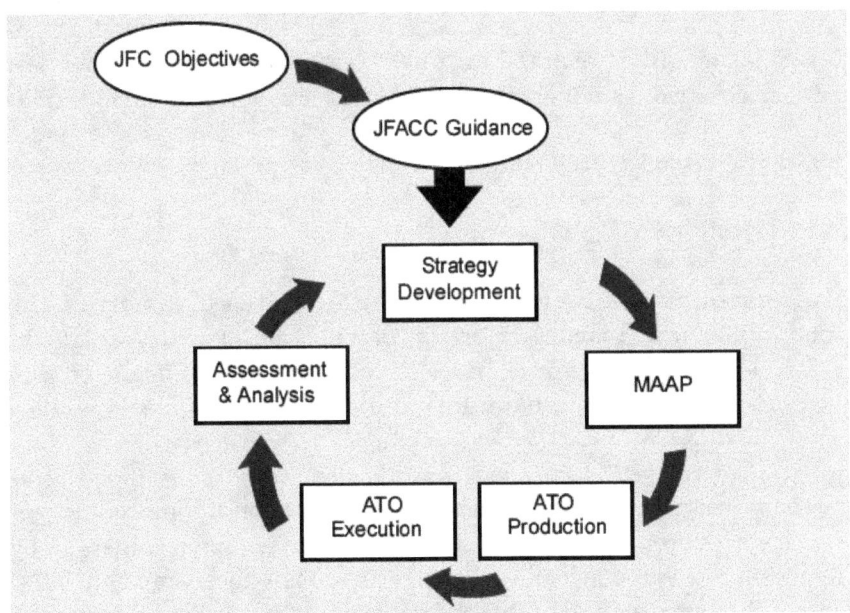

**Figure 3.1. Nominal ATO Development Cycle**

The ATO cycle provides for the continuous collection, correlation, and prioritization of a variety of relevant inputs, in accordance with the JFC's intentions. The cycle also provides a repetitive process for planning, coordination, allocation, execution, and assessment of air missions. The cycle accommodates changing tactical situations, the JFC's revised priorities and objectives, and requests for support from other Service and functional commanders in an air tasking directive, which is the ATO. The ATO incorporates specific targets compiled by the JAOC staff with the availability and capability of forces provided to the JFACC for the given ATO day. The cyclic ATO transmits mission tasking to individual units, normally each day. The ATO is a detailed document specifying numbers of sorties, refueling tracks and times, targets, times over target (TOT), ordnance, coordinating and controlling agencies, as well as communications frequencies. In many situations, the JFACC issues mission type orders (MTO) to assigned and attached air units. MTOs state the objectives to be accomplished but leave the detailed mission planning to the tasked units. This enables subordinate echelons to exploit fleeting opportunities better. Mission type orders can help the JFACC reduce "micro-management" when developing and transmitting an ATO. JFACCs pass along required planning information to units via SPINS and the ACO and normally include their commander's intent as part of the ATO. Tactical unit commanders and flight leaders determine the tactics employed to accomplish the missions at the unit level, using decentralized orders. *This represents the "decentralized execution" vital to aerospace flexibility.* A less detailed ATO is required for units collocated with each other that have established coordination procedures for mission planning. If units are geographically separated or do not have reliable and secure communications, more detailed coordination may be required in the ATO.

## APPORTIONMENT

**Apportionment is the determination and assignment of the total expected aerospace effort by percentage, priority, weight of effort, or some other appropriate means, that should be devoted to the various aerospace operations and geographic operations for a given period of time.** *The JFACC normally makes an apportionment recommendation to the JFC, based on the overall needs of theater strategy and the available aerospace forces.* JFCs normally apportion by priority or percentage of effort into geographic areas, against mission type orders, or by functional or mission categories significant for the campaign. JFC approval of apportionment sets the degree of effort dedicated to accomplishing specific missions. For example, when opposed by an enemy with a credible air force or missile threat, air superiority becomes a prerequisite for successful military operations. In this case, the JFC normally apportions a larger percentage of air assets to counterair missions during the initial stages of the conflict than in other circumstances. Apportionment may remain relatively constant during an individual phase of a campaign or require frequent adjustment when several phases of the campaign are conducted simultaneously.

## TARGET DEVELOPMENT

**Once the available aerospace forces have been apportioned into broad categories, a more detailed process develops the specific targets that will be attacked to achieve aerospace objectives, thereby supporting the overall strategy.** Target development takes place in the JAOC, normally as a part of the combat plans function. All potential targets are prioritized and selected for inclusion on the joint integrated prioritized target list (JIPTL) based on intelligence recommendations, component requests, "no hit" lists, collection priorities, and other factors. All components and agencies involved in or supported by aerospace operations have an input in this process through both the target request process and the component liaisons to the JAOC. If the JFC decides to convene a joint targeting coordination board (JTCB) then that body will provide additional broad targeting guidance to help ensure the consistency of aerospace targeting with overall theater strategy. *The key for including a target on the JIPTL is a demonstrated link between that target's destruction and the achievement of aerospace and overall military objectives.* A sample JIPTL is included in Appendix D.

## ALLOCATION AND WEAPONEERING

**Once the apportionment decision is made, the JFACC allocates resources to accomplish specific missions.** Mission packages are normally constructed to get the most from the available resources. The master air attack plan (MAAP) and the ATO provide more detailed guidance on how daily aerospace operations will be conducted.

### Master Air Attack Plan

The MAAP provides theater level sequencing and resource inputs necessary for producing an ATO and is the first time in the air tasking process that detailed resource availability is matched against specific targets. The following factors, while not all inclusive, represent the primary considerations for developing the MAAP. A brief sample of a generic MAAP is in Appendix E.

○ **Time Relationships Inherent in Aerospace Objectives and Tasks.** The JAOP envisions a certain chain of events which seeks to increase the vulnerability of enemy targets, increase the options available to friendly forces, and minimize the attrition of friendly forces. The JAOP should therefore consider probable enemy reactions and build flexibility into any projected sequence of objectives and tasks. Some objectives and tasks do not require a particular sequence; in such cases, operations occur simultaneously with a weight of effort to reflect the JFACC's and JFC's intent. At the air campaign level, phasing allows the JFACC to prioritize and sequence events; the air campaign also guides prioritization and sequencing of objectives and tasks within each phase.

○ **Target-based Timing Requirements.** The relative values of targets depend on their contributions to an enemy's capacity to function governmentally, militarily, or economically. The characteristics of targets may also dictate the assignment of timing requirements to their order of attack in the MAAP. For instance, some targets are time-critical because not striking them first might allow the enemy an opportunity to inflict unacceptable losses on friendly forces. Other targets are of a fleeting nature; while their destruction may not be critical to success on the first day of the war, that may be the only time they can be targeted. As an example, mobile targets are more readily targeted in garrison than after they are dispersed. Several other factors concerning individual targets may drive timing requirements, such as the need for immediate battle damage assessment, the desire to limit collateral damage, or unique intelligence which relates the value and vulnerability of a target to a specific time.

○ **Synergies to Minimize Losses and Achieve Decisive Results.** As a general rule, stealth, standoff weapons (to include cruise missiles), and specialized SEAD assets are used to degrade C2, EW/ground control intercept (GCI), and lethal air defenses, providing less stealthy aircraft greater freedom of maneuver. At the tactical level, surprise is important, mass is useful, and unpredictability a healthy option when considering the principles of war to decrease the friendly loss rate to enemy air defenses. While risk of losses drives the sequence of employing specialized assets to a great extent, events on the ground or near an area of concentrated attack may also dictate the order of attack. Air campaign plans may mass aircraft to maximize the protection afforded by limited

SEAD or OCA assets and exploit transitory weaknesses in enemy defenses. Another example of massing is attacking targets that are close together, even though they support different objectives.

○ **Effects of Other Joint Operations.** Support to ground or naval forces may dictate the order of attack for a portion of the MAAP. The MAAP should have the flexibility to adapt to the changing battlefield situation throughout the theater. The MAAP also adjusts to the changing availability of other joint assets to ensure each task or target is assigned the best available capability. As a minimum, planners should track availability of missile and airborne assets of the other components or Services. However, aerospace planners should be careful not to confine their planning to air and space assets alone, as the integration of surface maneuver units or special forces units in support of certain aerospace objectives can produce decisive results.

○ **Availability of Friendly Air Assets.** While this factor is critical in determining the desired sequence in the MAAP, it should not be the only one. Indeed, the availability of aircraft, weapons, skilled personnel, and support assets will limit the number of attacks in any one period of time as well as the number of certain types of targets that can be struck simultaneously. However, these considerations should fine tune the MAAP sequence, and not be the foundation for it. Consideration of friendly force availability provides a feasibility check for the MAAP so that AOC planners may readily translate it into an ATO.

**Weaponeering**

All approved targets are weaponeered on target worksheets, which detail recommended aimpoints (otherwise known as desired mean points of impact [DMPIs]), recommended number and type of aircraft and weapons to achieve the desired level of effect, weapons fusing, target identification and description, target area terrain (desert, jungle, urban, etc.), target area threats and weather, and restrictions on collateral damage. Weapons selection should also take into account the availability of the various weapons being considered. *Certain high value weapons, such as those capable of deep penetration, are normally limited in number and should only be used against those targets that both require the weapon for successful attack and that have a definitive value to the enemy.* In some cases such as CAS or armed reconnaissance, the specific target will not be known during the planning process. For these missions, weaponeering should provide those munitions that have broad effectiveness against all the likely targets that may be encountered.

# AIR TASKING ORDER (ATO) DEVELOPMENT

After the MAAP is approved by the JFACC, detailed preparations continue on the joint ATO, SPINS, and ACO. JFC and JFACC guidance, target worksheets, the MAAP, and various component inputs are used to finalize the ATO, SPINS, and ACO. Components may submit critical changes to target requests and asset availability during this final phase of joint ATO development; such changes will likely end up as amendments and not as part of the original ATO. The ACA and AADC instructions should be provided in sufficient detail to allow components to plan and execute all missions tasked in the joint ATO. These directions should enable combat operations without undue restrictions, balancing combat effectiveness with the safe, orderly, and expeditious use of airspace. ACA instructions should provide for quick coordination of task assignment or reassignment. The AADC should direct aircraft identification and engagement procedures and ROE that are appropriate to the nature of the threat and existing constraints. ACA and AADC instructions should also consider the volume of friendly air traffic, counterair requirements, identification, friend or foe (IFF) technology, weather, and enemy capabilities. ACA and AADC instructions are contained in monthly, weekly, and daily SPINS, and also in the ACO that is updated as frequently as required. The joint ATO, ACO, and SPINS provide operational and tactical direction at appropriate levels of detail. These documents should be very explicit when forces operate from different bases and multicomponent or composite missions are tasked. By contrast, less detail is required when missions are tasked to a single component or base. A sample ATO is shown in Appendix F.

# THEATER AIR CONTROL SYSTEM

**The JFACC normally employs the TACS to plan, direct, and control theater air operations.** The TACS consists of both ground and airborne elements and is directly involved in the command and control of most air missions. The TACS has the capability to plan, direct, coordinate, and control all air operations, including air defense and airspace control, and to coordinate for required space mission support. The size and structure of the TACS is tailored to meet theater-specific needs determined by the JFACC. The structure of the TACS should reflect sensor coverage, component liaison elements, and the communications required to provide adequate support. The TACS consists of the JAOC and subordinate air and ground control elements. In multinational commands, the name

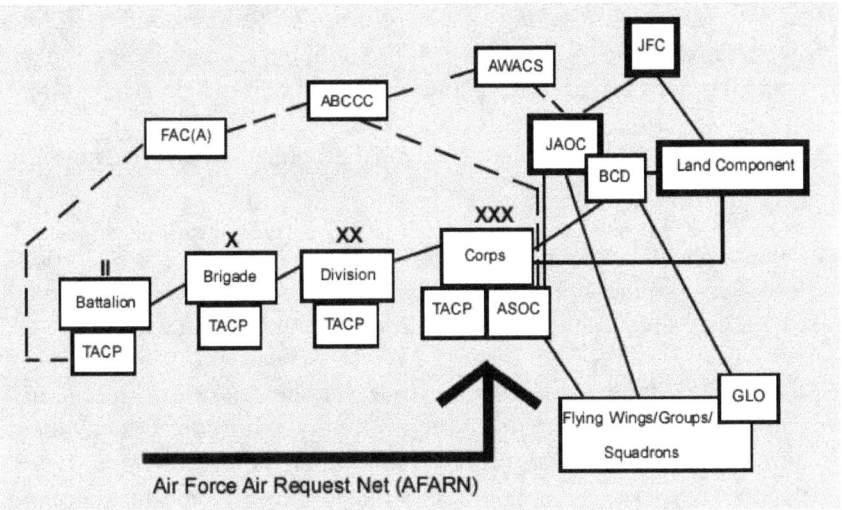

**Figure 3.2. The US Air Force TACS System**

and function of certain TACS elements may differ, but multinational air components have similar capabilities.

## Joint Air Operations Center (JAOC)

The JAOC is the JFACC's planning and execution headquarters. The JAOC is responsible for centralized planning, direction, control, and coordination of aerospace operations. The JFACC is normally designated as the AADC and ACA, so these functions are typically performed at the JAOC as well. The JAOC monitors execution of air operations and directs changes as the situation dictates. As the focal point of the TACS, the JAOC should have secure and redundant communications with operations, logistics, weather, and intelligence centers, higher and lateral headquarters, as well as subordinate units to preclude degradation in its ability to control air forces. Primary functions of the JAOC include:

⊘ Receiving, assembling, analyzing, filtering, and disseminating all-source intelligence and weather information. Intelligence and weather personnel work within Combat Plans and Combat Operations Divisions to provide direct support for ATO development and execution.

⊘ Developing an air campaign strategy for future operations to meet JFACC objectives and guidance and building supporting planning documents that implement the air strategy.

- Acting for the ACA, issuing airspace control procedures, and coordinating airspace control activities. This includes transmitting airspace control orders and activating joint special operations areas (JSOAs).

- Acting for the AADC, providing overall direction of defensive counterair, including theater missile defense.

- Directing and controlling execution of day-to-day aerospace operations. Providing rapid reaction, positive control, coordinated and deconflicted weapons employment, as well as integration of the total air effort.

- Conducting combat assessment to determine mission results (battle damage assessment), reattack requirements, munitions effectiveness, and overall air campaign effectiveness as required by the JFC to support the theater combat assessment effort. This effort supports higher-level operational and strategic assessment, which in turn helps guide campaign execution.

- Establishing procedures within the JAOC for modifying the current ATO in light of emerging threats, battle damage assessment results, or changes in guidance.

- Integrating the IO effort to achieve a synergistic plan for the JFACC. The IO effort within the JAOC does this by interfacing with the intelligence and target planning functions.

**Other Centers and Liaison Elements**

**Other centers and elements within the JAOC provide coordination with the other Service components, as well as interface for other functional components such as special operations and combat search and rescue.** Liaison elements provide senior level interface for supported land, maritime, and special operations forces. Appropriate liaison elements are established within the JFACC's staff to coordinate efforts of theater air assets. These liaison elements should have adequate communications with their respective Service component commands to support informed decisions regarding the use and sustainability of their force's assets.

### Ground Elements

**Ground-based elements of the TACS, subordinate to the JAOC, provide similar capabilities as airborne elements but with reduced range, flexibility, and mobility.** However, ground-based elements do not depend on high-value assets for continuous operations. Additionally, they offer an important interface between the TACS and ground-based air defense activities. Ground TACS responsibilities are often delegated to the control and reporting center (CRC) and air support operations center (ASOC).

✪ **Control and Reporting Center.** The CRC is the senior element responsible for decentralized execution of air defense and airspace control functions. The CRC:

   ✪✪ Performs identification and surveillance of assigned area of operations.

   ✪✪ Monitors both offensive and defensive missions and provides threat warning.

   ✪✪ Manages airspace and air defense.

   ✪✪ Coordinates control of missions with subordinate elements and other agencies.

✪ **Control and Reporting Element (CRE).** The CRE is subordinate to the CRC and augments the CRC's mission by extending radar surveillance and airspace control capabilities within a CRC's assigned area of responsibility. In a system environment, one CRE will normally be designated as the alternate CRC. The CRE:

   ✪✪ Provides aircraft control in the forward area.

   ✪✪ Provides early warning and surveillance.

   ✪✪ Provides gap-filler radar coverage.

   ✪✪ Provides forward-deployed data link interface with other agencies.

⊙ **Air Support Operations Center.** The ASOC is the element responsible for planning, coordination, control, and execution of air operations that directly support ground combat forces. ASOCs are normally located at corps level. In multicorps theaters, each corps fire support element (FSE) will be collocated with an ASOC. Each ASOC reports to the JAOC. On-scene OPCON of the ASOC is maintained by the corps air liaison officer (ALO), who is normally the ASOC director during operational contingencies or exercises. The ASOC:

✪✪ **Provides Air Force expertise to senior Army tactical echelons.** Advises the ground commander on the capabilities and limitations of aerospace power. ASOC personnel should provide expertise on how and when air operations can enhance the effectiveness of ground operations, allowing objectives to be achieved at less cost. ASOCs should include ground force intelligence and operations representatives, as well as appropriate liaison personnel of other components.

✪✪ Collocates with the senior tactical FSE and provides control of air support allocated by the JAOC to the aligned ground combat unit. Act as the corps ALO's conduit for CAS requests by controlling and maintaining the Air Force air request net (AFARN).

✪✪ Forwards ground forces' requests for airborne electronic warfare (EW) support and Air Force requests for ground or heliborne EW support.

✪✪ Exercises OPCON of subordinate tactical air control parties (TACPs) aligned with ground force combat units subordinate to the corps.

✪✪ Coordinates joint air attack team (JAAT) missions that employ helicopters together with fixed-wing assets.

⊙ **Tactical Air Control Parties.** TACPs are subordinate to the ASOC and are the single points of direct Air Force interaction with supported ground combat units. Each combat maneuver battalion, brigade, division, and corps headquarters will have an aligned TACP. Combat aviation (attack only) brigades will also have an aligned TACP. TACPs are staffed with ALOs and other terminal attack controllers. They conduct liaison and control functions appropriate to the level of combat maneuver force supported. ALOs, Enlisted Tactical Air Controllers

**Tactical air control parties provide on-scene command and control, taking maximum advantage of airpower's flexibility by directing strikes where they are most needed.**

(ETAC), tactical air command and control specialists/technicians (TACCS), and forward air controller (airborne) [FAC(A)s] are the only personnel authorized to perform terminal control of CAS aircraft during operations (combat and peacetime) within close proximity of their supported ground combat units.

○ **Wing Operations Centers (WOC).** *WOCs are the staff headquarters for each flying wing.* Wing commanders and their staffs receive orders, directives, and guidance from the JAOC through the WOC. WOCs manage resources, plan missions, and direct operations for their respective wings. Composite wing WOCs may perform appropriate JAOC duties for planning and execution of the air war when deployed or operating independently. WOCs also monitor and control local surface-to-air missile (SAM) and antiaircraft artillery (AAA) operations on and immediately around airbases.

Airborne Elements

**Airborne elements of the TACS provide a highly responsive, flexible, and survivable system to support the execution and coordination of theater aerospace operations.** They may be employed autonomously during the early stages of theater contingencies and conflict or in concert with multinational and joint Service command and control systems. As demonstrated during DESERT STORM, airborne elements of the TACS can rapidly react to changing situations by adjusting sensor and communications coverage to support ATO execution. As the technology for direct sensor-to-shooter links provide more options for aerospace force application, C2 and battle management techniques should grow to properly exploit those options. Airborne elements rely on onboard systems as well as direct connectivity with off-board intelligence collectors (such as RC-135 RIVET JOINT) to accurately assess the combat arena and adjust force execution. The JFACC augments the airborne battlestaff with direct representation having the authority to modify the ATO. Airborne elements of the TACS include:

○ **Airborne Battlefield Command and Control Center (ABCCC).** The ABCCC supports aerospace operations by coordinating air support with land force elements. It serves as an airborne ASOC or as the extension of the ground-based ASOC. The ABCCC has the capability of supporting command and control of SOF missions or serving as an extension of the Combat Operations Division of the JAOC.

○ **Airborne Warning and Control System (AWACS).** AWACS provides the TACS a highly survivable airborne radar platform. AWACS is normally one of the first assets to arrive in any new theater of operations. It establishes an initial C2 capability and provides early warning, radar surveillance, battle management, and weapons control functions. AWACS provides detection and control of low-level aircraft beyond the coverage of ground-based radars. AWACS will normally carry an airborne battlestaff or airborne command element (ACE) authorized to redirect forces under the authority of the JFACC. AWACS can assign weapons to engage threat targets, scramble and divert aircraft conducting counterair missions, detect and identify hostile airborne targets, and recommend changes in air defense warning conditions.

○ **Joint Surveillance, Target Attack Radar System (JSTARS).** JSTARS is a joint Air Force/Army system designed to provide surveillance, target detection, and target-tracking capability to develop a picture of the enemy surface situation. It is used to provide updates on enemy force disposition, identify opportunities for rapid interdiction and retargeting of enemy ground forces, and can also perform some battle management functions.

**Advanced technologies, like JSTARS, continue to improve our information capability, optimizing airpower's effect.**

✪ **Forward Air Controller (Airborne) [FAC(A)].** The FAC(A) provides terminal control for CAS aircraft operating in close proximity to friendly ground forces. The FAC(A) is the only person cleared to perform such control from the air, and can be especially useful in controlling CAS against targets that are beyond the visual range of friendly ground forces.

*Once mastery of the air was obtained, all sorts of enterprises would become easy.*

**Sir Winston Churchill**

# CHAPTER FOUR

# TRAINING AND EDUCATION FOR AIR WARFARE

*The Battle of Waterloo was won on the playing fields of Eton.*

**Lord Wellington**

If the above quotation is indeed true, then it would be just as valid to state that DESERT STORM was won at the Nellis ranges and the US Army's National Training Center (NTC). Throughout history proper preparation of warriors for battle has included the technical details of practicing tactics—the planning experience to produce winning strategies and the human element of exposure to realistic battlefield conditions. Actions over Bosnia and Kosovo again reinforced the lessons of realistic training at both the operational and tactical levels of war.

## TRAINING FACTORS

**Thorough training is vital for success in all aspects of aerospace operations.** The ability to plan and execute a theater air campaign requires the same rigorous preparation required to achieve tactical excellence. Training, therefore, involves mastering the necessary level of knowledge and then developing the judgment to use that knowledge in the fog of war. Training enables the timely and coordinated completion of many difficult and diverse tasks required by a JFACC and the JFACC's staff during the conduct of theater air warfare. Realistic training prepares air forces to transition from peace to war and back. Commanders at all levels are responsible for training and preparing forces for their wartime mission. Individuals should learn and practice their wartime tasks prior to the outbreak of hostilities. The pace of modern warfare may not allow time to polish skills, develop new procedures and techniques, or create new organizational structures as the crisis develops or after hostilities begin. Hence, training for aircrews, battle staff, and support personnel should be as realistic as possible to reinforce the will as well as the skill of the airman.

## BATTLE MANAGEMENT TRAINING

**At the heart of effective C2 for air forces is the battle management function.** The goal for battle management training is to have component staffs train with the same realism and intensity that exercises such as RED FLAG provide for aircrews. Just as aircrews face realistic threats in getting to the target, commanders and air component planners need to experience the stresses of selecting targets and devising concepts of operations in plausible and realistic scenarios. Campaign planning, combat staff expertise, and C2, are critical to warfighting—they make it possible to strike the right target with the most appropriate system. Training for this crucial aspect of warfare is conducted through specialized training programs and exercises. In addition to molding existing battle staffs into smooth operating teams, these programs ensure that personnel sent to augment battle staffs in theater commands have been trained to perform effectively, immediately upon arrival. Proper training exposes planners to the environment they will be thrust into, should the situation arise, with very little warning.

> *I have flown in just about everything, with all kinds of pilots in all parts of the world—British, French, Pakistani, Iranian, Japanese, Chinese—and there wasn't a dime's worth of difference between any of them except for one unchanging fact: the best, most skillful pilot had the most experience.*
>
> **Charles E. ("Chuck") Yeager**

## AIRCREW TRAINING

**Experience in war and peacetime tests shows effectiveness and aircrew survivability increase dramatically with combat experience.** The peacetime training goal is to provide the equivalent of combat experience in the maximum quantity and quality that resources can support. Operational ranges are central to this effort. The primary objective of operational ranges is to provide realistic training and testing areas. The combat environment, in terms of weather and its effects, surface and airborne targets, enemy air defenses, and general fog and friction, should be as realistic as training constraints allow. Computer simulations are used to enhance realism since a realistic environment for training contributes directly to increased combat effectiveness.

Operational academic training can be an important means of getting knowledge gained from combat experience out to the field. While not a substitute for hands-on experience, academics are valuable and should be included in every unit's training program.

## EXERCISES AND WARGAMING

**Exercises should be planned and conducted in a way that reflects real war.** For example, if large-scale force packages in a given scenario would include threat suppression aircraft, then such aircraft need to participate in exercises. Since some of the most effective operations occur at night, night training should be as thorough and intensive as daytime training. To improve readiness, air, space, and information forces, including airlift, participate in numerous large-scale exercises at home and overseas. JCS-directed exercises strive to improve joint interoperability of procedures through field exercises for aircrews and command post exercises for staffs. Exercises in overseas locations provide realistic training for in-theater air forces programmed for deployment to those locations. These exercises allow forces to gain valuable experience in the joint and multinational combat environments. Not only do aerospace forces need to participate in exercises, they need to do it smartly and jointly to ensure we *train the way we fight.*

**Exercises at all levels of war need to maintain a proper focus.** Over experimentation with either operational or tactical doctrine does not help the operators. Most experimentation is best left to battlelabs or those exercises specifically designated "experimental;" doing otherwise results in planners and operators who do not have a solid basis of knowledge and experience to build on during wartime. *Likewise, honesty and accuracy in after-action reports are critical in today's environment of high operations tempo and reduced time available for in-depth exercising.*

**Wargaming** is used by both the Air Force and the military in general for training, education, and testing new concepts for employment and organization. *It is critical that aerospace power be properly represented in wargames, as it is fundamentally different from ground and sea power and should be modeled accordingly.* Where ground combat wargames often focus on force-on-force attrition models with acceptable results, such an approach for aerospace power ignores the primary methods of force application historically used in combat. Aerospace planners normally seek to attack key COGs or other critical targets that cause large-scale disruption of the enemy force, thus avoiding the more costly and much longer process of destroying the enemy one tank or truck at a time. If the wargame does not adequately reflect this approach, then it will teach the wargamers the wrong lessons about aerospace power's strengths, limitations, and desired methods of employment.

# A Primer on Major US Air Force and Joint Exercises

This section briefly describes a few major USAF and joint exercises by providing the objective, method, and participants of each exercise. It is not intended to be all encompassing, rather, the primer provides a brief overview to help form an airman's knowledge base.

## FLAG EXERCISES:

RED FLAG is a realistic combat training exercise employing the air forces of the US and its allies on the vast bombing and gunnery ranges at Nellis AFB NV, Air Warfare Center (AWFC) through the 414th Combat Training Squadron.

The "Blue" forces use various tactics to attack Nellis range targets: mock airfields, vehicle convoys, tanks, parked aircraft, bunkered defensive positions, missile sites, etc. These targets are defended by a variety of simulated ground and air threats to give participating aircrews the most realistic combat training possible.

GREEN FLAG is similar to a RED FLAG but emphasizes intelligence gathering, bomb damage assessment, and electronic warfare.

MAPLE FLAG is a combined US/Canadian Flag exercise held at Canadian Forces Base (CFB) Cold Lake, Canada. Units fly as a combined air package through the Primrose Lake range. This exercise provides a chance for units to exercise with a full mix of allied participants in a NATO atmosphere.

BLUE FLAG increases Air Combat Command's (ACC) readiness by providing battle staff experience to number air force (NAF) and other selected personnel in a realistic environment. Training emphasizes the activities needed to plan and execute operations in accordance with current tasked theater war plans (when able). BLUE FLAG is ACC's foremost large scale, force-on-force, computer-assisted, airpower exercise.

## ROVING SANDS:

The primary focus of ROVING SANDS is joint tactical air operations (JTAO). The exercise location is western Texas and southern New Mexico, primarily in the White Sands Missile Range (WSMR) and Fort Bliss, TX areas. Theater missile defense (TMD) has become a very important facet of ROVING SANDS. Commander in Chief, US Joint Forces Command (USCINCJFCOM) theater missile defense initiative (TMDI) operates in conjunction with ROVING SANDS.

## AIR WARRIOR I (AW):

Air Warrior provides realistic close air support (CAS), air interdiction (AI), and airborne forward air control (FAC[A]) training in a simulated brigade-level conflict conducted at the US Army's National Training Center (NTC).

Air Warrior integrates elements of Air Land Battle training at NTC with combat air and theater air control system elements. Theater air control system improvements through CAS/AI training result from a realistic simulated combat environment. The ground war is fought at Ft Irwin CA and the air battle is flown from Nellis AFB NV.

## AIR WARRIOR II (AWII):

Air Warrior II is designed to provide realistic CAS, AI, and airborne forward air control (FAC(A)) training, in a simulated low to mid intensity conflict at the US Army's Joint Readiness Training Center (JRTC). Air Warrior II provides light infantry battalion-sized unit commanders and their staff a data source for improving tactics and procedures and theater air control system improvements through CAS/AI training in a realistic simulated combat environment. The ground war is fought at Ft Polk LA, and the air battle is flown from Barksdale AFB LA.

**UNIFIED ENDEAVOR (UE):**

UE is a US Joint Forces Command (USJFCOM) exercise designed to train a joint task force (JTF) commander/staff and JTF component commanders/staffs on joint task force operations. In accordance with USJFCOM's JTF training program, the focus is on joint academic training; standing up a JTF; crisis action planning procedures; joint doctrine; and tactics, techniques and procedures application. The JTF is comprised of Army, Air Force, Navy, Marine and special operations forces (SOF). The commander, JTF develops an operations order (OPORD) and then conducts operations based on that order as directed by USCINCJFCOM.

**INTERNAL LOOK:**

Internal Look is a US Central Command (USCENTCOM)-directed battle staff exercise designed to train a JTF commander/staff. The focus is on command and control training; standing up a JTF; crisis action planning procedures; joint doctrine; and tactics, techniques and procedures application. The JTF will be comprised of Army, Air Force, Navy, Marine and SOF components of US CENTCOM. The CJTF develops an OPORD and then conducts operations based on that order as directed by Commander in Chief, US Central Command (USCINCCENT).

**JOINT TASK FORCE EXERCISE (JTFEX):**

JTFEX is a CJCS-approved, USJFCOM-scheduled, component-sponsored, field training exercise employing Army, Air Force, Navy, Marine Corps, and SOF elements in a littoral environment off the east coast of the United States. The exercise is conducted to support requirements-based joint interoperability training for USJFCOM forces and to certify the participating Carrier Battle Group (CVBG) and Amphibious Ready Group (ARG)/Marine Expeditionary Unit (MEU) for forward deployment.

# EDUCATION

**The Air Force has a number of education programs that prepare the airman to better employ aerospace power.** They are designed to increase professional knowledge and, more broadly, to improve critical thinking skills and develop analytical ability. Different programs are applicable at various points throughout an airman's career and are most effective if accomplished at the appropriate time.

## Professional Continuing Education (PCE)

**PCE is designed to increase an airman's knowledge of important concepts in a particular area of expertise.** A number of commands and schools offer courses specifically designed to improve the conduct of air warfare. Some courses, such as the *Joint Doctrine Air Campaign Course,* are designed to help planners and commanders understand the planning and command and control of aerospace operations. Others, such as some courses offered by the US Air Force Special Operations School, focus on a particular means of employing aerospace power. PCE programs are effective once an airman has developed the basic skills necessary to perform the air warfare mission.

## Professional Military Education (PME)

PME provides broad education appropriate for different points in an officer's, noncommissioned officer's (NCO), or civilian's career. Within these programs, airmen learn about Air Force doctrine and the role of aerospace power in joint doctrine. An understanding of doctrine is critical if aerospace power is to be effectively employed in operations and properly represented in the joint arena. Sequential levels of PME provide the student a broader doctrinal foundation with which to operate.

## Graduate Education

Graduate education programs, both military and civilian, provide the knowledge and the perspective that help airmen apply tactical skills, plan operations, and prepare for the future. Liberal arts programs such as military history or international relations help airmen understand the context in which air warfare will be conducted. Technical programs such as engineering or the physical sciences may help airmen develop new tools that match the tenets of aerospace power with emerging technologies.

Air University at Maxwell AFB provides a continuum of education that helps prepare airmen for leadership, command, staff, and management responsibilities.

*At the Very Heart of Warfare lies Doctrine. . .*

# Suggested Readings

Armitage, M.J. and Mason, R.A., *Air Power in the Nuclear Age* (University of Illinois Press). 1985.

Byman, D. L., Waxman, M. C., and Larsen, E., *Air Power as a Coercive Instrument* (Rand). 19996.

Clausewitz, Carl von, *On War* (Princeton University Press). 1976.

Corbett, Julian S., *Some Principles of Maritime Strategy* (Navy Institute Press). 1988.

Creveld, Martin Van, *Command in War* (Harvard University Press). 1985.

Hosmer, Steven T., *Psychological Effects of U.S. Air Operations in Four Wars, 1941-1991* (Rand). 1996.

Jomini, Antoine Henri de, *The Art of War* (Greenhill Books). 1996.

Lambert, Andrew P.N., *Psychological Effects of Airpower* (RUSI). 1994.

Liddell-Hart, B.H., *Strategy* (Meridian). 1991.

Mason, Tony, *Airpower: A Centennial Appraisal* (Brassey's). 1994.

Pape, Robert A., *Bombing to Win* (Cornell University Press). 1996.

Sun Tzu, *The Art of War* (Westview Press). 1994.

Warden, John, *The Air Campaign* (Presidio Press). 1989.

Warden, John, *The Enemy as a System* (Airpower Journal). Spring 1995.

Wylie, J. C., *Military Strategy* (Navy Institute Press). 1989.

# APPENDIX A

# THE STRATEGIC APPRECIATION

1. **Context.** The first step is to assess the strategic context of the conflict. This requires an in-depth assessment of enemy and friendly sources of national power. The examples and categories that follow are illustrative, not exhaustive.

    a. Enemy strategic analysis: This analysis promotes an understanding of enemy interests and objectives. Effective control of the adversary leadership and associated power structure is the key to achieving strategic goals.

        (1) Political strengths, weaknesses, and trends such as:

- Commitment of enemy powers to their alliance.
- Additional potential allies and their vital interests.
- Strength of central government, method of rule (by mandate, terror, or both).
- General distribution of power: centralized or decentralized (legislative, military, security, financial, press, and tribal organizations and elites).
- Political frailties.

        (2) Social strengths, weaknesses, and trends such as:

- Assessment of national values.
- Dominant political or religious ideologies.
- Societal arrangements along religious, ethnic, tribal, or political lines.
- Commitment or obedience to national or ethnic leadership.

        (3) Information flow factors such as:

- Control of media.
- Reliance on verbal, written, radio, and television media.
- Public access to television and radio.
- Potential influence of international media on the enemy's internal public support.

(4) Economic dependencies, sources of national power a
and trends such as:

- ✪ Industry/agriculture/transportation systems.
- ✪ Energy and water sources.
- ✪ Reliance on international trade and imports of critical raw materials,
- ✪ Banking, credit and import routes.

(5) Military strengths, weaknesses, and trends such as:

- ✪ Force structure (conventional/unconventional).
- ✪ Proficiency and readiness.
- ✪ Sustainability and survivability.
- ✪ Doctrinal tendencies.
- ✪ Nuclear, biological, and chemical (NBC) weapons and delivery capability.
- ✪ Terrorist capability within the theater of operations or US.

b. Assess the friendly strategic situation using the same variables listed above. This should help the planner identify possible friendly strategic weaknesses and COGs.

2. **Enemy and Friendly Objectives.** Enemy objectives may have to be deduced—avoid accepting their stated objectives at face value. From a friendly perspective, ideally the NCA and the JFC will set national- and theater-level objectives. When this is the case, it is advantageous to restate higher-level objectives verbatim. Realistically though, objectives are often ambiguous, especially early in the campaign planning process. Because of this, planners often have to infer national objectives. Even if strategic guidance is not clear or specific, military objectives should be written to clearly convey what the campaign is designed to achieve.

3. **Assumptions.** Explicitly state assumptions the campaign depends on. The most important ones are often the hardest to state. These may include expectations about public reaction, weather, training, willingness of the enemy to use weapons of mass destruction, duration of the campaign, and enemy reaction. It is important to remember that the US and its enemies often do not share the same value system.

4. **Capabilities.** Compare absolute physical capabilities with limitations in training, adaptability, friction, and confusion to get a feel for realistic capabilities of both sides.

5. **Costs.** Assess what costs each national decision-making authority can bear in money, casualties, equipment and force structure, and political influence.

6. **Conclusion.** If the strategic appreciation is easy, straightforward, and certain, it probably has been rushed. The greatest value of this effort is that it clarifies the complex strategic environment of the theater. A solid understanding of the strategic environment lays a firm foundation for the whole air campaign planning process.

# APPENDIX B

# THE AIR ESTIMATE OF THE SITUATION

1. **Objective(s).** State the objective(s) assigned by higher authority or deduced from instructions from that source. These are usually stated from the point of view of the theater commander and should have a defined, measurable purpose. In every case the first duty of a commander receiving a mission is to be satisfied that he understands what is required of his command as a part of the larger team.

   a. National Objectives. Overarching goals of the United States as articulated by the National Command Authorities.

   b. Supported Theater Objectives. Objectives developed by the theater commander to achieve the national objective.

   c. Assigned Aerospace Objectives. Objectives specifically assigned to the JFACC by the JFC or those objectives which the JFACC can assume that are required to conduct air operations. Each course of action developed has its own specific objectives.

2. **Situation and Courses of Action.** This step develops several courses of action that can be taken by air and space forces. Each course should be substantially different in some respect. One course may use interdiction as the primary means to destroy the enemy's fielded forces, whereas in another it may only serve as a supporting function. Any course of action should not only support the JFC's objectives but also consider the desired end state as well (e.g., destructively or nondestructively disable an electrical power station). Either might support the JFC's objectives, but might have very different end state effects. All courses of action should include logistics considerations. Another method to differentiate courses of action is to change the phasing of air operations.

   a. State commander's intent:

      (1) Identify desired end-state.

      (2) Describe underlying logic for strategy (blueprint or pattern).

   b. State military objectives. For each objective:

      (1) State the objective clearly.

      (2) State how the objective supports theater and NCA objectives.

      (3) Specify tasks to be achieved and associated standards of performance.

c. Force assumptions (critical in a force projection scenario into an immature theater):

    (1) Total air forces potentially available to support course of action (Air Force, SOF, Navy, Marine, Army aviation and air defense artillery).

    (2) Reconnaissance assets required, both national and theater.

    (3) Surface forces required to support the course of action.

d. Estimate requirements:

    (1) Sorties and munitions required (by type aircraft where appropriate) to accomplish each task.

    (2) Time required to accomplish each task given the priority and phasing of the task.

    (3) Time permitting, sketch out the MAAP. NOTE: Both d(1) and d(2) have been traditionally underestimated.

    (4) Essential supporting tasks from other components (air base protection, logistical support, maneuver to support interdiction).

e. Logistics required to support:

    (1) Deployment schedule and strategic lift requirements [time-phased force and deployment data (TPFDD)]

    (2) Daily logistics requirements (POL, weapons, water, spare parts).

    (3) Intratheater lift requirements, both surface and air.

f. Force capabilities and ratios. Consider the order of battle for both sides.

    (1) Friendly Forces. Factors to be considered are:

        (a) Air/Space.

- ✪ Order of battle for air and space forces (include forces from other services and coalition nations made available to the JFACC for tasking).
- ✪ Operating capacity of friendly airfields.
- ✪ State of supply (POL, weapons, water) and replacements.
- ✪ Effect of weather on flying and sortie generation capability.

✪ Logistics support available from allies/ other Services (POL, water, surface transportation).

✪ Range of friendly aircraft and refueling capabilities.

(b) Ground/Naval.

✪ Order of battle. (Specify type—mechanized, light infantry, etc.)

✪ Coalition, and those SOF forces not under the control of the JFACC.

✪ Flow of forces into theater.

✪ Organic air defense capability.

✪ Availability of air and sea ports of debarkation.

✪ Potential naval operating areas.

(2) Enemy Forces. Consider, from the enemy viewpoint, factors similar to those given in (1) above.

(a) Command, control, and communications (C3).

(b) Air/Space.

✪ Air, air defense, and space order of battle.

✪ Operating and reconstitution capacity of enemy air fields.

✪ Effect of weather on flying and sortie generation capability.

✪ Logistics support available and lines of communication.

✪ Range of enemy aircraft and refueling capabilities.

✪ Mobile and fixed missile forces.

(c) Ground/Naval.

✪ Order of battle (specify type).

✪ NBC weapons, delivery capability, and manufacturing capability.

✪ Organic air defense capability.

✪ Potential naval operating areas.

(3) Relative Combat Strength. Compare the opposing forces to friendly forces from the point of view of the factors indicated above, and also from the point of view of physical condition,

morale, amount of recent operations, doctrine, training, and combat experience.

    (a)  Air Forces.

- ✪ Friendly forces' ability to conduct offensive air operations. Consider their ability to counter IADS from a technological and aircrew proficiency standpoint.
- ✪ Enemy ability to conduct offensive air operations
- ✪ Enemy and friendly ability to conduct air and space reconnaissance operations

    (b)  Land Forces.

- ✪ Based on the friendly current force structure and the planned force structure.
- ✪ Ability of enemy to conduct offensive operations.
- ✪ Vulnerability of friendly forces to air interdiction

    (c)  Maritime Forces.

- ✪ Friendly forces' ability to gain and maintain sea control in theater and for strategic lines of communication.
- ✪ Friendly forces' general vulnerability to air and sea threats.

  g.  Air component course of action. State all feasible and acceptable courses of action open to the commander that can potentially accomplish the mission.

3. **Analysis of Opposing Courses of Action.** The air component commander next assesses the intangible or abstract factor: the skill of the enemy commander. It is rarely possible to obtain direct information on the enemy's objectives, at least in time to use this information. Since they are a vital factor in the outcome, it is often necessary to deduce them.

  a.  Enemy Air/Space Options. State concisely the reasonable alternatives that the enemy air forces may adopt to oppose the air component commander's mission. Given that it is impossible to foresee or construct the actual plan that the enemy air commander follows, therefore all reasonable and probable hostile alternatives for his employment of airpower should be concisely stated and considered.

b. Enemy Ground/Naval Situation. Identify all reasonable surface force courses of action that would support their objectives. Include guerrilla force options.

c. Enemy NBC Options. Include likely delivery options (aircraft, terrorist, artillery, cruise missile, ballistic missile).

d. Analyses of Enemy Alternatives. Analyze each alternative given above and determine if it is workable and what its advantages and disadvantages might be. State whether each alternative has a reasonable chance of success and whether it would accomplish the enemy's probable objective if successful. In analyzing each potential enemy alternative, it is important to maintain the enemy's point of view.

e. Most Probable Courses of Enemy Action. Identify the alternatives available to the enemy which appear most suited to the enemy's probable intention. Include justification. When no one hostile plan appears to have a pronounced advantage over the others from the enemy viewpoint, select the one that seems most disadvantageous to friendly forces.

4. **Comparison of Own Courses of Action.** Compare each friendly course of action with each enemy course of action given above and determine if it workable and what its advantages are over its disadvantages, to include logistics considerations. Determine likely enemy responses to each friendly course of action. For each friendly course of action assess its chance of success, whether it would accomplish the strategic objectives if successful, and whether it would favor future action from the air commander and supporting forces.

5. **Decision.** The last step of the estimate, the DECISION, states the JFACC's recommended course of action. Normally, the JFACC proposes this course of action to the JFC. When it is approved, it becomes the JFACC's mission and the basis for the subsequent air campaign plan.

# APPENDIX C

# SAMPLE JOINT AIR OPERATIONS PLAN FORMAT

Copy No.
Issuing Headquarters
Place of Issue
Date/Time Group of Signature

JOINT AIR OPERATIONS PLAN: (Number or Code name)

REFERENCES: Maps, charts, and other relevant documents.

COMMAND RELATIONSHIPS: Briefly describe the command organization (composition and relationships) for the JFC's campaign and the aerospace operations envisaged. Detailed information may be included in the command relationships annex. Cover component commanders, Area Air Defense Commander (AADC) and Airspace Control Authority (ACA) identities, and others as required.

1. **Situation:** Briefly describe the situation that the plan addresses (see JFC's estimate). The related CONPLAN or OPLAN should be identified as appropriate.

    a. **Guidance:** Provide a summary of directives, letters of instructions, memoranda, treaties, and strategic plans, including any campaign/ operations plans received from higher authority, that apply to the campaign.

        (1) Relate the strategic direction of the JFC's requirements.

        (2) List strategic objectives and tasks assigned to the command.

        (3) Constraints—list actions that are prohibited or required by higher authority (ROE and others as appropriate).

    b. **Adversary Forces.** Provide a summary of pertinent intelligence data including information on the following:

        (1) Composition, location, disposition, movements, and strengths of major adversary forces that can influence action in the AOR/JOA.

        (2) Strategic concept (if known), should include adversary's perception of friendly vulnerabilities and adversary's intentions regarding those vulnerabilities.

        (3) Major objectives (strategic and operational).

        (4) Adversary commander's idiosyncrasies and doctrinal patterns.

(5) Operational and sustained capabilities.

(6) Vulnerabilities.

(7) Centers of gravity and decisive points.

c. **Friendly Forces.** State here information on friendly forces not assigned that may directly affect the command.

(1) Intent of higher, adjacent, and supporting US commands (e.g., USTRANSCOM, USSTRATCOM, USSOCOM, USSPACECOM).

(2) Intent of higher, adjacent, and supporting allied or other coalition forces (e.g., NATO, Spain, Italy, Egypt, etc.).

d. **Assumptions.** State here assumptions applicable to the plan as a whole. Include both specified and implied assumptions.

2. **Mission.** State the joint aerospace task(s) and the purpose(s) and relationship(s) to achieving the JFC's objective(s).

3. **Aerospace Operations.**

a. **Strategic or Operational Concept.** (Based on the relevant elements of the JFC strategy.) State the broad concept for the deployment, employment, and sustainment of major aerospace capable joint forces including the concepts of deception and psychological operations during the operation or campaign as a whole. (This section is a summary of details found in the annexes.)

(1) Joint aerospace force organization.

(2) Joint force aerospace objectives.

(3) Beddown overview.

(4) Operational missions.

(5) Phases of joint aerospace operations in relation to JFC operation or campaign plan.

(6) Timing and duration of phases. (Aerospace operations normally do not lend themselves to linear, sequential phasing. However, the concept of phases, even those conducted simultaneously or unparallel, might provide a useful framework for thinking about the attainment of intermediate objectives.)

b. **Phase 1.** Provide a phase directive for each phase.

(1) Operational concept. Include operational objectives, plan of attack, and timing.

(2) General missions and guidance to subordinates and components' supporting and supported requirements. Ensure that missions are complementary.

    (3) Capabilities/forces required by role or capability. Should consider land, sea, air, space, special operations, and multinational.

    (4) Tasks of subordinate commands and components.

    (5) Reserve Forces. Location and composition. State "be prepared" missions. Include guidance on surge sorties if used as reserve capability.

    (6) Mobility. Consider transportation, ports, lines of communication, transit and overflight rights, reinforcement, reception and onward movement, and host-nation support arrangements.

    (7) Deception.

    (8) Psychological Operations. Ensure joint aerospace operations will support established psychological operations.

  c. **Phases II to XX (last).** Cite information as stated in subparagraph 3b above for each subsequent phase, to include whether or not it will be conducted simultaneously with other phases. Provide a separate phase for each step in the operation at the end of which a major reorganization of forces may be required and another significant operation initiated.

  d. **Coordinating Instructions.** If desired, instructions applicable to two or more phases or multiple events of the command may be placed here.

4. **Logistics.** Brief, broad statement of the sustainment concept for the joint aerospace operations with information and instructions applicable to the joint aerospace operations by phase. Logistics phases must be consistent with operational phases. This information may be listed separately and referenced here. This paragraph should address:

  a. Assumptions.

  b. Supply aspects.

  c. Maintenance and modifications.

  d. Medical Service.

  e. Transportation.

  f. Base development.

  g. Personnel.

  h. Foreign military assistance.

  i. Administrative management.

  j. Line(s) of communication.

k. Reconstitution of forces.

l. Joint and multinational responsibilities.

m. Sustainment priorities and resources.

n. Inter-Service responsibilities.

o. Host-nation considerations.

5. **Command, Control, and Communications.**

   a. **Command.**

      (1) Command relationships. State generally the command relationships for the entire joint aerospace operations or portions thereof. Indicate any transfer of forces contemplated during the joint aerospace operations, indicating the time of the expected transfer. These changes should be consistent with the operational phasing in paragraph 3. Give location of commander, JAOC, and command posts.

      (2) Delegation of Authority.

   b. **Communications.**

      (1) Communications. Plans of communications. (May refer to a standing plan or contained in an annex.) Include time zone to be used; rendezvous, recognition, and identification instructions; code; liaison instructions; and axis of signal communications as appropriate.

      (2) Electronics. Plans of electronics systems. (May refer to standard plan or may be contained in an annex.) Include electronic policy and other such information as may be appropriate.

      (3) Combat Camera. Plans for combat camera. (May refer to standard plan or may be contained in an annex.) Include digital still photo and motion video imagery transmission to the Pentagon's Joint Combat Camera Center.

      (4) Armament Delivery Recording (ADR) (bomb and gun camera imagery). Plan for ADR. (May refer to a standard plan or may be contained in a combat camera annex.) Include imagery transmission to the Pentagon's Joint Combat Camera Center.

      (5) Communications and Information Requirements: Determine, resource, and integrate supporting communications and information systems, personnel, and necessary bandwidth to meet joint aerospace operational requirements.

(Signed) (Commander)

ANNEXES: As required.

# APPENDIX D

# SAMPLE JOINT INTEGRATED PRIORITIZED TARGET LIST (JIPTL)

| Target | # | RANK | PREV |
|---|---|---|---|
| Destroy attacking enemy surface forces in contact | G2 1 | 1 | 1 |
| C2 of enemy air defense forces in ZOC 3 and ZOC 4 | A2 1 | 2 | 2 |
| Destroy advancing enemy operational reserve heavy units | 02 3 | 3 | 9 |
| Disrupt logistics support of enemy operational reserve | 02 4 | 4 | 19 |
| Attrit advancing enemy 1st/2d echelon divisions by 50% | H2 3 | 5 | 3 |
| Destroy enemy artillery attacks on Phantom airfield | A2 5 | 6 | 5 |
| Disrupt C2 of enemy operational reserve | 02 2 | 7 | 8 |
| Support JFMC maritime superiority operations | M2 1 | 8 | 10 |
| Degrade enemy ISR assets | I2 2 | 9 | 18 |
| Degrade enemy air to ground fighter capability | A2 4 | 10 | 13 |
| Degrade enemy air superiority fighter capability | A2 3 | 11 | 14 |
| Destroy enemy TBM capability | A2 6 | 12 | 15 |
| Destroy enemy radar guided SAM threat vic PMF | A2 2 | 13 | 16 |
| Attrit helicopter units supporting enemy advance | H2 4 | 14 | 17 |
| Shape/delay enemy operational reserve advance toward PMF | 02 1 | 15 | 20 |
| Disrupt C2 of enemy 1st/2d echelon divisions | H2 2 | 16 | 21 |
| Disrupt logistics support of enemy 2d echelon divisions | H2 5 | 17 | 11 |
| Shape/delay enemy ground force advance | H2 1 | 18 | 12 |
| Deny enemy use of space based navigation | S2 6 | 19 | 22 |

# APPENDIX E

# SAMPLE MASTER AIR ATTACK PLAN

## Master Air Attack Plan

| TOT | MSN# | TGT | DESCRIPTION | AIRCRAFT |
|---|---|---|---|---|
| H-15 | 63819 | A011 | COMMAND POST | 1 F-117 |
| H-10 | 6302C | A09 | ALERT FIELD | 2 F-117 |
| 0000 | 6554D | AS034 | AIRCRAFT FUEL | 4 F-15E |
| 0000 | 43821 | SAD32 | EW/GCI PLATFORM | 4 F-16 |
| 0000 | 43822 | N/A | AREA SEAD | 4 EA-6B |
| 0000 | 43823 | N/A | AREA/HVA CAP | 4 F-14 |
| 0000 | 5103R | AR71 | AAR TRACK | 3 KC-135R |
| 0025 | 0255U | CCC01 | NATIONAL C2 | 2 F-117 |
| 0000 | 33717 | INT37 | RAILROAD BRIDGE | 4 Tornado |
| 0115 | 3212A | INT16 | POL STORAGE | 2 F-15E |
| 0125 | 2714G | CP A4 | CAS | 4 A-10 |

# APPENDIX F

# SAMPLE AIR TASKING ORDER

ATOCONF MESSAGE SETS (BREAKOUT KEY)
MSNDAT / MSNNO / PKG / CALLSIGN / NUMACTYPE / AMSN /
      ALRT / SCL1 / SCL2 / SIF1 / SIF2
MSNLOC / TIME ON STATION / TIME OFF STATION / LOCATION
      NAME / ALTITUDE / REQUEST NUM / LOCATION
TGTLOC / TIME ON TGT / TIME OFF TGT / TGT ID / TGT TYPE /
      DMPI / REQUEST / COMMENTS
CONTROL / TYPE / CALLSIGN / PRIMARY FREQ / SECONDARY
      FREQ / REPORT POINT / COMMENTS
FACINFO / CALLSIGN / PRIMARY FREQ / SECONDARY FREQ /
      REPORT POINT / SUPPORT UNIT ID / COMMENTS
ELECMBT / CALLSIGN / PRIORITY / LOCATION / ALTITUDE /
      TOS / TFS / PRIMARY FREQ / SECONDARY FREQ
RECDATA / REQUEST NUM / PRIORITY / TIME ON TGT / LTIOV /
      REC MSN TYPE / COVG TYPE / IMAGERY TYPE / IMG
QUALIFIER / COVG MODE / TGT CODE / PRINT SCALE /
DELIVER ADDRESS
TRCPLOT / INITIAL POINT / RADIUS, WIDTH OR ELLIPSE AND
      QUALIFIERS
REFUEL / TANKER CALLSIGN / TANKER MSNNO OR TANKER
      TACAN / ARCP / ALTITUDE / ARCT / OFFLOAD / TKR
      FREQ 1 / TKR FREQ 2
\*\*\*\*\*\*\*\*\*\*\*\*\*\*\*\*\*\*\*\*\*\*\*\*\*\*\*\*\*\*\*\*\*\*\*\*\*\*\*\*\*\*\*\*\*\*\*\*\*\*\*\*\*\*\*\*\*\*\*\*\*\*\*\*\*\*\*\*\*\*\*\*\*\*\*\*\*\*\*\*\*\*\*\*\*\*

ATO A: FAA000 UNCLAS EXER/ //
MSGID/ATOCONF//AOC//
PERID/OOOOOOZ/TO:OOOOOOZ//
AIRTASK/ATO A//
TASKUNIT/353TFS//
MSNDAT/AF003/-/GMAN11/4XA10A/GCAS/15M/A1/-/31511-//
TGTLOC/-/-/-/-//
AMPN/SEE UNIT REMARKS 1, 2, 3 ACEMAKER//
MSNDAT/AF004/-/GMAN15/4XA1OA/GCAS/15M/A1/-/31515/-//
TGTLOC/-/-/-/-//
AMPN/SEE UNIT REMARKS 1, 2, 3, ACEMAKER//
MSNDAT/AF005/-/GMAN21/4XA10A/GCAS/30M/A1/-/31521/-//
TGTLOC/-/-/-/-//
AMPN/SEE UNIT REMARKS 1, 2, 3, ACEMAKER//

MSNDAT/AF001/-/GMAN01/4XA1OA/CAS/-/A1/-/31501/-//
TGTLOC/121330Z/121350Z/B1234-12345/FTAFLD/
303645.7N1202739.1W/123B/BOMB DUMP//
AMPN/SEE UNIT REMARKS 1, 2, 3, ACEMAKER//
MSNDAT/AF002/-/GMAN05/4XA1OA/CAS/-/A1/-/31505/-//
TGTLOC/121530Z/121550Z/B123412345/FTAFLD/
303645.7N1202739.1W/124B/BOMB DUMP//
AMPN/SEE UNIT REMARKS 1, 2, 3, ACEMAKER//
TASKUNIT/59TFS//
MSNDAT/FT0011/-/GLIDER01/4XF15/DCA/-/D5/-/31401/-//
TGTLOC/-/-/-/-//
AMPN/SEE UNIT REMARKS 1, 2, 3 ACEMAKER//
MSNDAT/FT0015/-/GLIDER05/4XF15/DCA/-/D5/-/31405/-//
TGTLOC/-/-/-/-//
AMPN SEE UNIT REMARKS 1, 2, 3, ACEMAKER//
RMKS//

# APPENDIX G

# ADDITIONAL PLANNING TOOLS

This appendix presents a variety of various tools and models available for the aerospace planner. Some are more official in nature than others, but all have been used at various times in exercises, actual combat operations, or both.

Figure G.1. illustrates the interaction of external and internal elements and their relationship to the planing process.

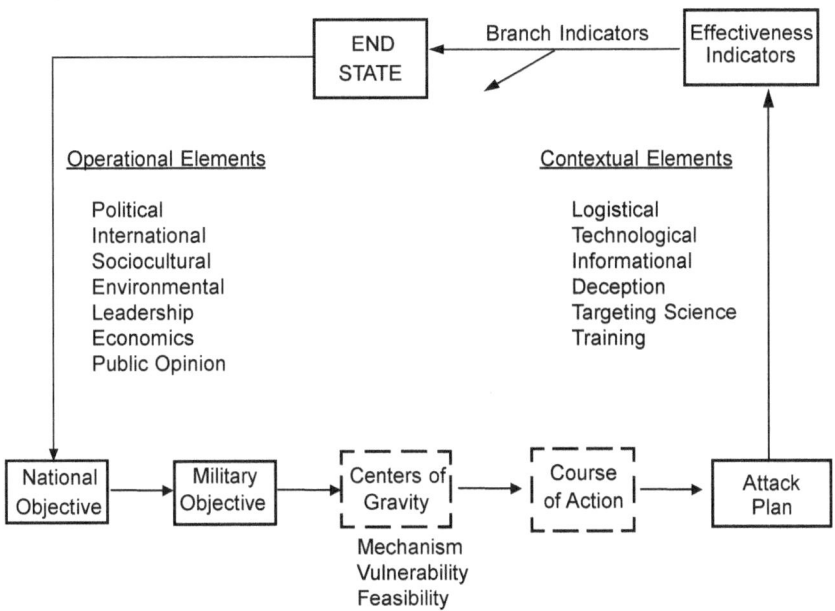

**Figure G.1. Contextual Elements Planning Model**

# TYING OBJECTIVE TO STRATEGY TO TASK

An important part of any military planning is ensuring that selected strategies and tasks support higher-level objectives. The following two models (figures G.2 and G.3) are often used to illustrate this concept for aerospace warfare planning:

Z-Diagram: Objective ⟶ Mechanism⟶ Strategy

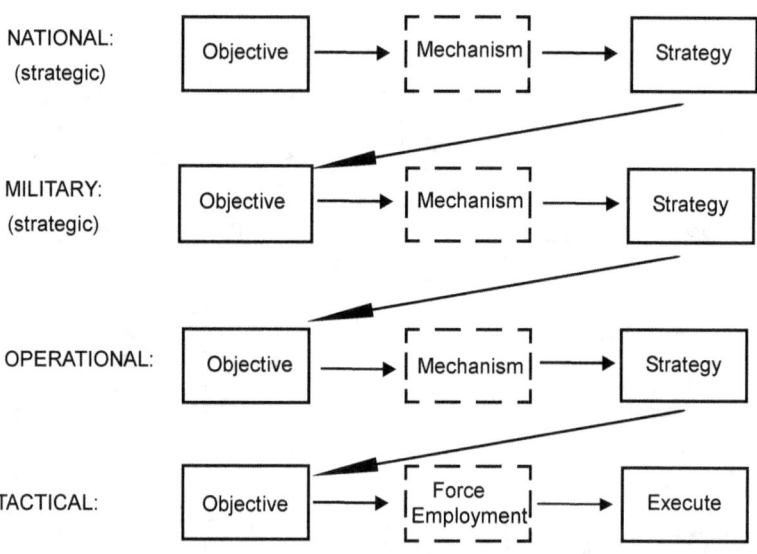

**Figure G.2. Z-Diagram**

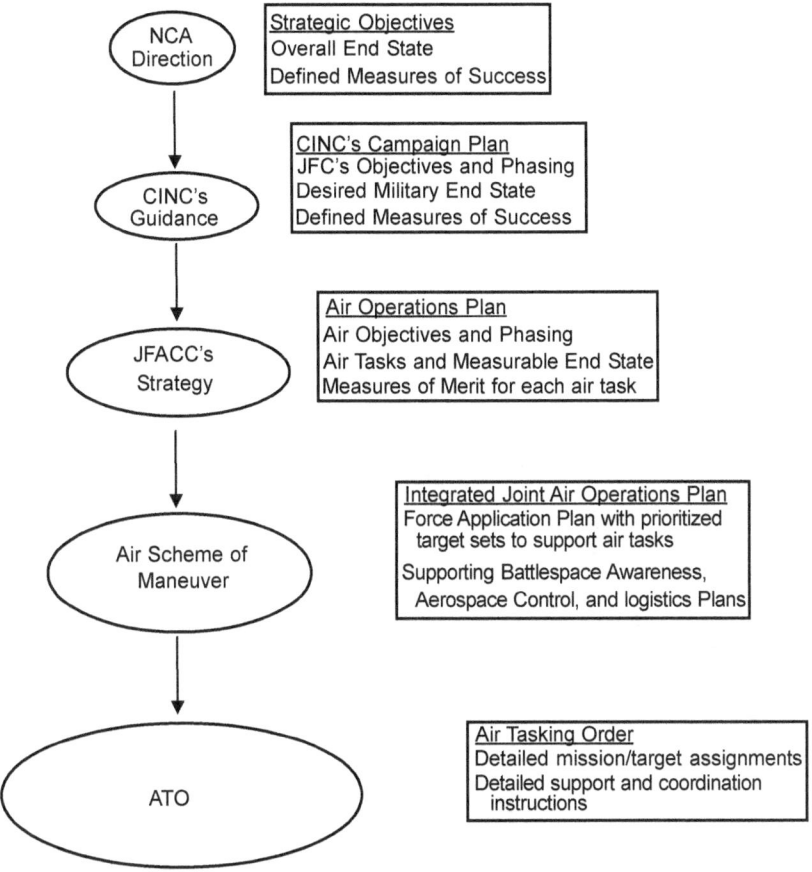

**Figure G.3. Strategy to Task for ATO Development**

# Center of Gravity Development

Figure G.4. shows the COG process from start to finish. Note that it must begin with national policy and military objectives and include assessment of operations to determine if the COG(s) should be adjusted as the operation progresses. The enemy may take actions that make the original COG no longer critical or develop such defensive or dispersion measures that new methods of attack are required.

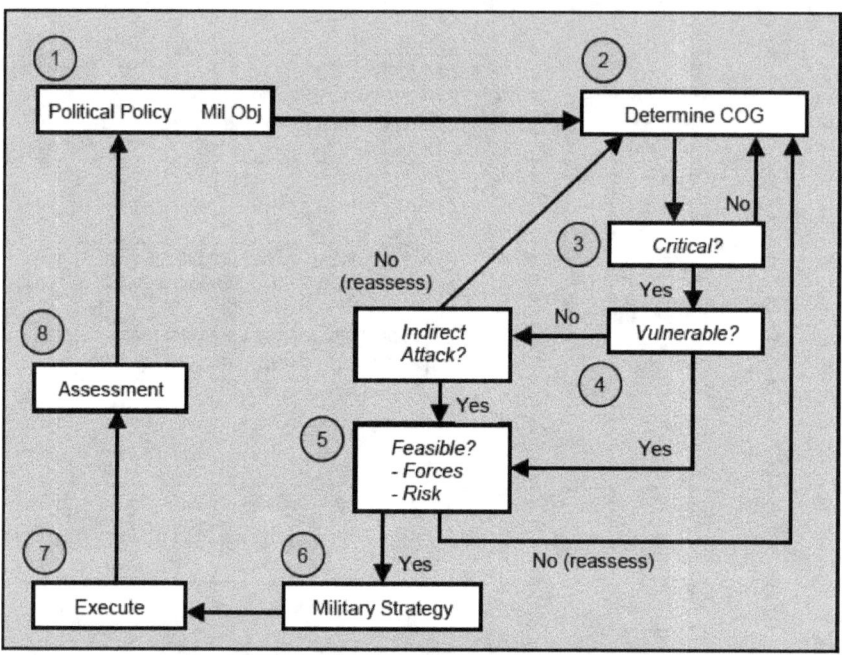

**Figure G.4. Center of Gravity Development**

1. Receive overall policy and military guidance from above.
2. Analyze the adversary for possible COGs.
3. Determine if candidate COGs are truly critical to the enemy strategy. This analysis must include a thorough examination of the mechanism by which COG influence will affect enemy strategy.
4. Determine if identified COGs or their linkages are vulnerable to direct attack. If not, examine for possible indirect attack.
5. Determine if the method of influencing the COG is feasible, considering such questions as number and quality of friendly forces, ROE, level of conflict, projected losses, etc.
6. Develop overall military strategy to support the military objectives. Among other factors, the strategy must consider objectives, threat, environment, mechanism, and law of armed conflict.

7. Execute the strategy and attack/influence the COG as part of the military operation.

8. Assess the success of the attack and study the overall impact on adversary strategy (operational and strategic assessment). Assess adversary reaction to the attack, and determine if follow-up attacks are required or if a new COG should be sought.

# Five-Ring Targeting Model

The five-ring model was developed as part of the "enemy as a system" concept, which analyzes the enemy from a systemic perspective. This model can be used for analyzing the enemy as a whole or specific portions of an enemy system may themselves be broken down into the five categories using the "rings within rings" approach. The model places leadership at the center based on the idea that leadership is normally the ultimate target and attacks to directly affect leadership, when possible, are often effective. How far the effects of disrupting leadership go towards achieving military and national objectives depends on a host of variables specific to each conflict.

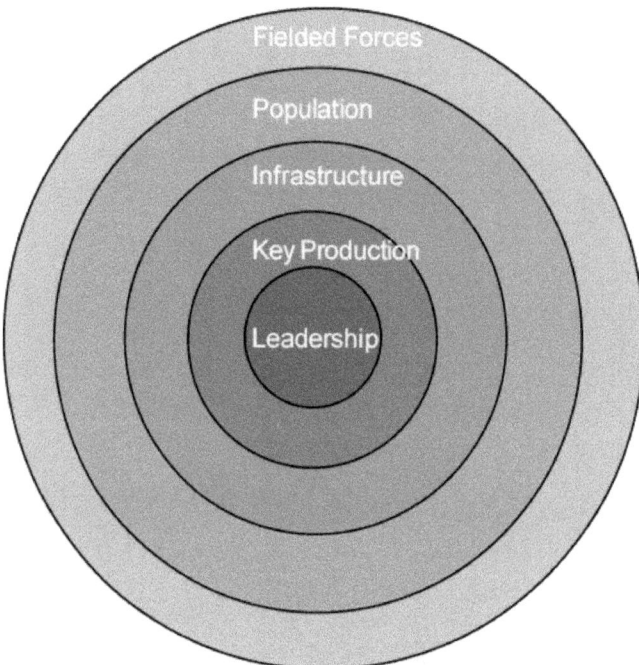

**Figure G.5. Five-ring Model**

A further development of the five-ring concept (see figure G.6) has been proposed which renames some of the categories and adds a "connectivity" outer ring to indicate the interaction between various nations, groups, or other actors.

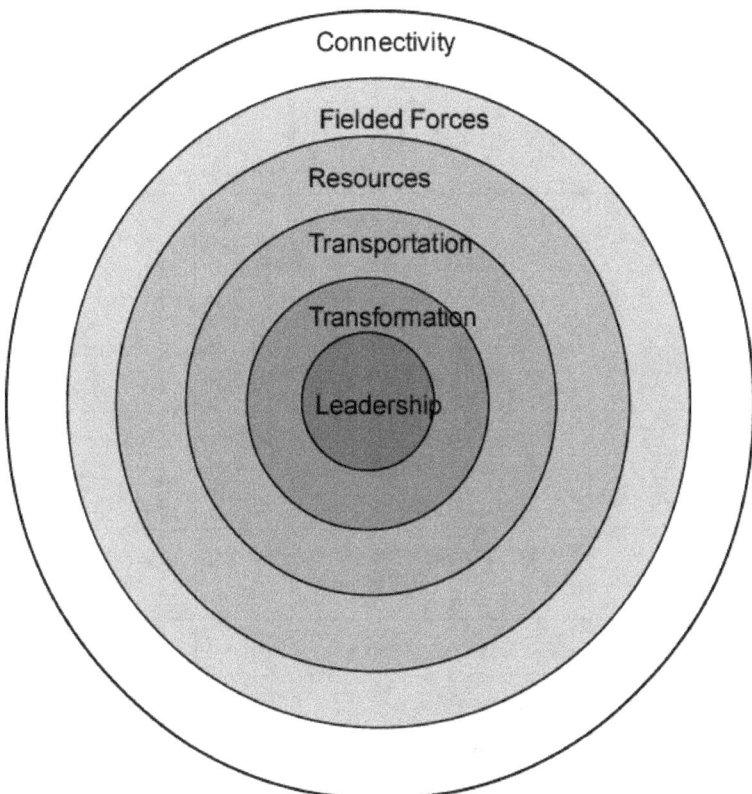

**Figure G.6. Six-ring Model**

Figure G.7 below presents two samples of this process, in this case using the six-ring method. The nation-state example provides a military campaign application while the human body example represents the concept's application against a familiar "system."

| Ring Label | Nation-State Example | Human Body Example |
|---|---|---|
| Leadership | Includes actual leaders, collection and analysis, doctrine, strategy, (the entire "decision-making" process) | Brain, sensors (eyes, ears, etc.) |
| Transformation | Engines, systems or processes that transform resources into other resources or products valuable to the overall system | Lungs, digestive system |
| Transportation | Transports resources, products or information from one location to another (rail, road, air transport, comm links, shipping, etc.) | Circulatory system, lymphatic system, trachea |
| Resources | Resources used by other rings within the system (human population, raw materials, etc.) | Air, water, food |
| Forces | Fielded combat forces, tactics, equipment and supplies *in the field* | White blood cells, antibodies |
| Connectivity | How the system influences or is influenced by the outside world(treaties, imports, exports, immigration, etc.) + *ENEMY FORCES* | Light waves, sound waves, invading germs |

**Figure G.7 Six-ring Method Process**

# Glossary

## Abbreviations and Acronyms

| | |
|---|---|
| AAA | antiaircraft artillery |
| AADC | area air defense commander |
| ABCCC | airborne battlefield command and control center |
| ACA | airspace control authority |
| ACC | Air Combat Command |
| ACE | airborne command element |
| ACO | airspace control order |
| ACP | airspace control plan |
| ADR | armament delivery recording |
| AEF | aerospace expeditionary force |
| AFAC | airborne forward air control |
| AFARN | Air Force air request net |
| AFB | Air Force Base |
| AFDD | Air Force doctrine document |
| AFSOF | Air Force special operations forces |
| AI | air interdiction |
| ALO | air liaison officer |
| AMC | Air Mobility Command |
| AO | area of operations |
| AOC | aerospace operations center |
| AOR | area of responsibility |
| ARG | Amphibious Ready Group |
| ASOC | air support operations center |
| ATACMS | Army Tactical Missile System |
| ATO | air tasking order |
| AW | Air Warrior |
| AWII | Air Warrior II |
| AWACS | airborne warning and control system |
| AWFC | Air Warfare Center |
| | |
| BCD | battlefield coordination detachment |
| | |
| C2 | command and control |
| C3 | command, control, and communications |
| CAS | close air support |
| CFB | Canadian Forces Base |
| CINC | commander in chief |

| | |
|---|---|
| CJCS | Chairman, Joint Chiefs of Staff |
| CJTF | commander, joint task force |
| COA | course of action |
| COCOM | combatant command (command authority) |
| COG | center of gravity |
| COMAFFOR | Commander, Air Force Forces |
| CONPLAN | operation plan in concept format |
| CONUS | continental United States |
| CRC | control and reporting center |
| CRE | control and reporting element |
| CSAR | combat search and rescue |
| CVBG | carrier battle group |
| | |
| DCA | defensive counterair |
| DCS | defensive counterspace |
| DMPI | designated mean point of impact |
| | |
| EA | electronic attack |
| EP | electronic protection |
| ES | electronic warfare support |
| ETAC | enlisted terminal attack controller |
| EW | electronic warfare |
| | |
| FAC(A) | forward air controller (airborne) |
| FACP | forward air control post |
| FSE | fire support element |
| | |
| GCI | ground control intercept |
| GLO | ground liaison officer |
| GPS | global positioning system |
| | |
| HARM | high-speed antiradiation missile |
| HUMINT | human intelligence |
| | |
| IADS | Integrated Air Defense System |
| ICBM | intercontinental ballistic missile |
| IFF | identification, friend or foe |
| IMINT | imagery intelligence |
| IO | information operations |
| IPB | intelligence preparation of the battlespace |
| ISR | intelligence, surveillance, and reconnaissance |

| | |
|---|---|
| JAAT | joint air attack team |
| JFACC | joint force air component commander |
| JAOC | joint air operations center |
| JAOP | joint air operations plan |
| JFC | joint force commander |
| JFSOCC | joint force special operations component commander |
| JIPTL | joint integrated prioritized target list |
| JOA | joint operations area |
| JPEC | Joint Planning and Execution Community |
| JRTC | Joint Readiness Training Center [US Army] |
| JSOA | joint special operations area |
| JSOACC | joint special operations air component commander |
| JSCP | Joint Strategic Capabilities Plan |
| JSTARS | joint surveillance, target attack radar system |
| JTAO | joint tactical air operations |
| JTCB | joint targeting coordination board |
| JTF | joint task force |
| JTFEX | joint task force exercise |
| | |
| LOAC | law of armed conflict |
| | |
| MAAP | master air attack plan |
| MAGTF | Marine air-ground task force |
| MAJCOM | major air command |
| MEU | Marine Expeditionary Unit |
| MOOTW | military operations other than war |
| MTO | mission type orders |
| | |
| NAF | numbered air force |
| NATO | North Atlantic Treaty Organization |
| NBC | nuclear, biological, and chemical |
| NCA | National Command Authorities |
| NCO | noncomissioned officer |
| NTC | National Training Center [US Army] |
| | |
| OCA | offensive counterair |
| OCS | offensive counterspace |
| OPCON | operational control |
| OPORD | operation order |
| OPLAN | operations plans |

| | |
|---|---|
| OPR | office of primary responsibility |
| OSA | Operational Support Airlift |
| | |
| PJ | individual pararescue specialist |
| POL | petroleum, oils, and lubricants |
| POW | prisoner of war |
| PSYOP | psychological operations |
| | |
| ROE | rules of engagement |
| | |
| SAM | surface-to-air missile |
| SEAD | suppression of enemy air defenses |
| SIOP | Single Integrated Operation Plan |
| SOF | special operations forces |
| SPINS | special instructions |
| | |
| TACC | tanker airlift control center; tactical air control center |
| TACCS | tactical air command and control specialists/technicians |
| TACON | tactical control |
| TACP | tactical air control party |
| TACS | theater air control system |
| TLAM | TOMAHAWK land attack missiles |
| TMD | theater missile defense |
| TMDI | theater missile defense initiative |
| TPFDD | time-phased force and deployment data |
| | |
| UE | UNIFIED ENDEAVOR |
| USACOM | United States Atlantic Command |
| USCENTCOM | United States Central Command |
| USCINCACOM | Commander in Chief, US Atlantic Command |
| USCINCCENT | Commander in Chief, US Central Command |
| USCINCSPACE | Commander in Chief, US Space Command |
| USSOCOM | United States Special Operations Command |
| USSPACECOM | United States Space Command |
| USSTRATCOM | United States Strategic Command |
| USTRANSCOM | United States Transportation Command |
| | |
| WMD | weapons of mass destruction |
| WOC | wing operations center |
| WSMR | White Sands Missile Range |

## Definitions

**aerospace.** Of, or pertaining to, Earth's envelope of atmosphere and the space above it; two separate entities considered as a single realm for activity in launching, guidance, and control of vehicles that will travel in both entities. ( JP 1-02)

**air superiority.** That degree of dominance of the air medium which permits the conduct of operations by friendly land, sea, and air forces at a given time and place without prohibitive interference by the enemy, while denying that enemy the same freedom of action.

**airspace control authority.** The commander designated to assume overall responsibility for the operation of the airspace control system in the airspace control area. Also called **ACA.** ( JP 1-02)

**allocation.** In a general sense, distribution of limited resources among competing requirements for employment. Specific allocations (e.g., air sorties, nuclear weapons, forces, and transportation) are described as allocation of air sorties, nuclear weapons, etc. See also allocation (air); allocation (nuclear); allocation (transportation); apportionment. ( JP 1-02)

**apportionment.** In the general sense, distribution for planning of limited resources among competing requirements. Specific apportionments (e.g., air sorties and forces for planning) are described as apportionment of air sorties and forces for planning, etc. See also allocation; apportionment (air). ( JP 1-02)

**area air defense commander.** Within a unified command, subordinate unified command, or joint task force, the commander will assign overall responsibility for air defense to a single commander. Normally, this will be the component commander with the preponderance of air defense capability and the command, control, and communications capability to plan and execute integrated air defense operations. Representation from the other components involved will be provided, as appropriate, to the area air defense commander's headquarters. Also called **AADC.** (JP 1-02)

**campaign plan.** A plan for a series of related military operations aimed at accomplishing a strategic or operational objective within a given time and space. ( JP 1-02)

**centers of gravity.** Those characteristics, capabilities, or localities from which a military force derives its freedom of action, physical strength, or will to fight. ( JP 1-02)

**close air support.** Air action by fixed- and rotary-wing aircraft against hostile targets which are in close proximity to friendly forces and which require detailed integration of each air mission with the fire and movement of those forces. Also called **CAS.** (JP 1-02)

**component.** One of the subordinate organizations that constitute a joint force. Normally a joint force is organized with a combination of Service and functional components. (JP 1-02)

**counterinformation.** Those actions dedicated to controlling the information environment.

**direct effect.** Result of actions with no intervening effect or mechanism between act and outcome. Direct effects are usually immediate and easily recognizable.

**electronic warfare.** Any military action involving the use of electromagnetic and directed energy to control the electromagnetic spectrum or to attack the enemy. Also called **EW.** The three major subdivisions within electronic warfare are: **electronic attack** — That division of electronic warfare involving the use of electromagnetic or directed energy to attack personnel, facilities, or equipment with the intent of degrading, neutralizing, or destroying enemy combat capability. Also called **EA.** EA includes: 1) actions taken to prevent or reduce an enemy's effective use of the electromagnetic spectrum, such as jamming and electromagnetic deception, and 2) employment of weapons that use either electromagnetic or directed energy as their primary destructive mechanism (lasers, radio frequency weapons, particle beams). **electronic protection.** — That division of electronic warfare involving actions taken to protect personnel, facilities, and equipment from any effects of friendly or enemy employment of electronic warfare that degrade, neutralize, or destroy friendly combat capability. Also called **EP.** and **electronic warfare support** — That division of electronic warfare involving actions tasked by, or under direct control of, an operational commander to search for, intercept, identify, and locate sources of intentional and unintentional radiated electromagnetic energy for the purpose of immediate threat recognition. Thus, electronic warfare support provides information required for immediate decisions involving electronic warfare operations and other tactical actions such as threat avoidance, targeting, and homing. Also called **ES.** Electronic warfare support data can be used to produce signals intelligence (SIGINT), both communications intelligence (COMINT) and electronics intelligence (ELINT). (JP 1-02)

**indirect effect.** Result created through an intermediate effect or mechanism to produce the final outcome, which may be physical or psychological in nature. Indirect effects tend to be delayed and may be difficult to recognize.

**information operations.** Actions taken to affect adversary information and information systems while defending one's own information and information systems. Also called **IO.** (AFDD 1)

**intelligence preparation of the battlespace.** An analytical methodology employed to reduce uncertainties concerning the enemy, environment, and terrain for all types of operations. Intelligence preparation of the battlespace builds an extensive data base for each potential area in which a unit may be required to operate. The data base is then analyzed in detail to determine the impact of the enemy, environment, and terrain on operations and presents it in graphic form. Intelligence preparation of the battlespace is a continuing process. Also called **IPB.** (JP 1-02)

**joint force air component commander.** The joint force air component commander derives authority from the joint force commander who has the authority to exercise operational control, assign missions, direct coordination among subordinate commanders, redirect and organize forces to ensure unity of effort in the accomplishment of the overall mission. The joint force commander will normally designate a joint force air component commander. The joint force air component commander's responsibilities will be assigned by the joint force commander (normally these would include, but not be limited to, planning, coordination, allocation and tasking based on the joint force commander's apportionment decision). Using the joint force commander's guidance and authority, and in coordination with other Service component commanders and other assigned or supporting commanders, the joint force air component commander will recommend to the joint force commander apportionment of air sorties to various missions or geographic areas. Also called **JFACC.** ( JP 1-02)

**operational assessment.** The measurement of effects at the operational level. Operational assessment determines whether or not force employment is properly supporting overall strategy by meeting operational objectives.

**operational control.** Transferable command authority that may be exercised by commanders at any echelon at or below the level of combatant command. Operational control is inherent in combatant command (command authority) (COCOM). Operational control may be delegated and is the authority to perform those functions of command over subordinate forces involving organizing and employing commands and forces, assigning tasks, designating objectives, and giving authoritative direction necessary to accomplish the mission. Operational control includes authoritative direction over all aspects of military operations and joint training necessary to accomplish missions assigned to the command. Operational control should be exercised through the commanders of subordinate organizations. Normally this authority is exercised through subordinate joint force commanders and Service and/or functional component commanders. Operational control normally provides full authority to organize commands and forces and to employ those forces as the commander in operational control considers necessary to accomplish assigned missions. Operational control does not, in and of itself, include authoritative direction for logistics or matters of administration, discipline, internal organization, or unit training. Also called **OPCON.** ( JP 1-02)

**operational effect.** Link between tactical results and strategy; typically the cumulative outcome of missions, engagements, and battles. Can also result from the disruption of systems or areas of operational value.

**operational level of war.** The level of war at which campaigns and major operations are planned, conducted, and sustained to accomplish strategic objectives within theaters or areas of operations. Activities at this level link tactics and strategy by establishing operational objectives needed to accomplish the strategic objectives, sequencing events to achieve the operational objectives, initiating actions, and applying resources to bring about and sustain these events. These activities imply a broader dimension of time or space than do tactics; they ensure the logistic and administrative support of combat forces, and provide the means by which tactical successes are exploited to achieve strategic objectives. ( JP 1-02)

**parallel attack.** Simultaneous attack of varied target sets to shock, disrupt, or overwhelm an enemy, often resulting in decisive effects. Parallel attack is possible at one or multiple levels of war and achieves rapid effects that leave the enemy little time to respond.

**strategic assessment.** The measurement of effects at the strategic level. Strategic assessment determines whether overall strategy is working and how well the strategic objectives of both sides are being achieved.

**strategic attack.** Military action carried out against an enemy's center(s) of gravity or other vital target sets, including command elements, war-production assets, and key supporting infrastructure in order to effect a level of destruction and disintegration of the enemy's military capacity to the point where the enemy no longer retains the ability or will to wage war or carry out aggressive activity. (AFDD 1)

**strategic effect.** Disruption of the enemy's overall strategy, ability, or will to wage war or carry out aggressive activity.

**strategic level of war.** The level of war at which a nation, often as a member of a group of nations, determines national or multinational (alliance or coalition) security objectives and guidance, and develops and uses national resources to accomplish those objectives. Activities at this level establish national and multinational military objectives; sequence initiatives; define limits and assess risks for the use of military and other instruments of national power; develop global plans or theater war plans to achieve these objectives; and provide military forces and other capabilities in accordance with strategic plans. ( JP 1-02)

**tactical control.** Command authority over assigned or attached forces or commands, or military capability or forces made available for tasking, that is limited to the detailed and, usually, local direction and control of movements or maneuvers necessary to accomplish missions or tasks assigned. Tactical control is inherent in operational control. Tactical control may be delegated to, and exercised at any level at or below the level of combatant command. Also called **TACON.** ( JP 1-02)

**tactical level of war.** The level of war at which battles and engagements are planned and executed to accomplish military objectives assigned to tactical units or task forces. Activities at this level focus on the ordered arrangement and maneuver of combat elements in relation to each other and to the enemy to achieve combat objectives. ( JP 1-02)

**theater air control system (TACS).** The organization and equipment necessary to plan, direct, and control theater air operations and to coordinate air operations with other joint component command and control agencies. It is composed of control agencies and communications-electronics facilities that provide the means for centralized control and decentralized execution of missions.

www.ingramcontent.com/pod-product-compliance
Lightning Source LLC
Chambersburg PA
CBHW070536290526
45790CB00002B/526